MAXnotes®

Aldous Huxley's

Brave New World

Text by
Sharon K. Yunker
(M.Ed., Xavier University)
Department of English
St. Bernard-Elmwood Place High School
St. Bernard, Ohio

Illustrations by
Karen Pica

Research & Education Association
Visit our website at
www.rea.com

Research & Education Association
61 Ethel Road West
Piscataway, New Jersey 08854
E-mail: info@rea.com

MAXnotes® for
BRAVE NEW WORLD

Published 2008

Copyright © 2003, 1995 by Research & Education
Association, Inc. All rights reserved. No part
of this book may be reproduced in any form
without permission of the publisher.

Printed in the United States of America

Library of Congress Control Number 2003100744

ISBN-13: 978-0-87891-751-8
ISBN-10: 0-87891-751-9

MAXnotes® and REA® are registered trademarks of
Research & Education Association, Inc.

E08

What **MAXnotes**® *Will Do for You*

This book is intended to help you absorb the essential contents and features of Aldous Huxley's *Brave New World* and to help you gain a thorough understanding of the work. Our book has been designed to do this more quickly and effectively than any other study guide.

For best results, this **MAXnotes** book should be used as a companion to the actual work, not instead of it. The interaction between the two will greatly benefit you.

To help you in your studies, this book presents the most up-to-date interpretations of every section of the actual work, followed by questions and fully explained answers that will enable you to analyze the material critically. The questions also will help you to test your understanding of the work and will prepare you for discussions and exams.

Meaningful illustrations are included to further enhance your understanding and enjoyment of the literary work. The illustrations are designed to place you into the mood and spirit of the work's settings.

This **MAXnotes** book analyzes and summarizes each section as you go along, with discussions of the characters and explanations of the plot. A biography of the author and examination of the work's historical context will help you put this literary piece into the proper framework of what is taking place.

The use of this study guide will save you the hours of preparation time that would ordinarily be required to arrive at a complete grasp of this work of literature. You will be well prepared for classroom discussions, homework, and exams. The guidelines that are included for writing papers and reports on various topics will prepare you for any added work that may be assigned.

The **MAXnotes** will take your grades "to the max."

Larry B. Kling
Chief Editor

Contents

> **Each chapter includes List of Characters, Summary,
> Analysis, Study Questions and Answers, and
> Suggested Essay Topics.**

MAXnotes® are simply the best – but don't just take our word for it...

"... I have told every bookstore in the area to carry your MAXnotes. They are the only notes I recommend to my students. There is no comparison between MAXnotes and all other notes ..."
– *High School Teacher & Reading Specialist,*
Arlington High School, Arlington, MA

"... I discovered the MAXnotes when a friend loaned me her copy of the *MAXnotes for Romeo and Juliet.* The book really helped me understand the story. Please send me a list of stores in my area that carry the MAXnotes. I would like to use more of them ..."
– *Student, San Marino, CA*

A Glance at Some of the Characters

John the Savage

The Director

Lenina Crowne

Henry Foster

Bernard Marx

Mustapha Mond

Helmholtz Watson

Linda

SECTION ONE

Introduction

The Life and Work of Aldous Huxley

Aldous Leonard Huxley was born in 1894 in Godalming, England. His father, Leonard, was a doctor and his mother, Julia, was the niece of the poet Matthew Arnold. At 16, Huxley contracted an eye disease, which caused him to endure blindness for three years and ended any possibility of a medical career. However, because of his family background and his own interests, his scientific training became an important part of his writing. He did state that he regretted missing some of that training during his blindness, training which, he said further, would be a necessity in order to live in the world of the twentieth century. As his blindness abated, he found he could read with the aid of a magnifying glass, and he managed to read well enough to earn his degree in English literature from Oxford University.

Huxley wrote across the literary spectrum: short stories, plays, nonfiction, and critical essays on topics ranging from art to literature to religion to censorship to poetry. His first book of poems, *The Burning Wheel,* was published in 1916 when he was 22 years old. Because of his vision problems, Huxley did not serve in World War I. He instead finished his university education and worked in a government office.

His early novels, such as *Crome Yellow* (1921) and *Antic Hay* (1923), contain criticisms of the British upper classes. Huxley said that the interruption of his own upper-class education had saved him from becoming one of those "proper English gentlemen." He married for the first time in 1919. For awhile, he and his wife lived in Italy, where he met and became a lifelong friend of the controversial D. H. Lawrence. Mark Rampion, a character in *Point Counter Point* (1928), is based on Lawrence.

Huxley moved to the United States in 1937, living in Taos, New Mexico and in California. His first wife died in 1955, and he remarried in 1956. He was fluent in four languages in addition to his native English, and he read Latin. He traveled widely, especially in Italy and France. His last novel, *Island*, was published in 1962. He was a contributing writer to several magazines, including *Life*, and he collaborated on several screenplays in Hollywood. He also wrote numerous critical essays and commentaries.

Aldous Huxley died in California in 1963. Many of his original manuscripts are at the University of California.

Historical Background

British life in 1932 was very different from American life. Almost an entire generation of men had been lost in World War I. Oxford University enrollment was only 491 in 1917, down from 3,181 in 1914. Among many of the upper-class poets and writers of the time—sometimes called the Auden Generation, after the poet W. H. Auden—there was a sense of disillusionment and futility. Britain's foreign investments had been depleted by war debts and loans. Higher living standards, prices, wages, and taxes became the order of the day in post-war Britain. By 1922, overpopulation had caused passage of the Empire Settlement Act to encourage and finance settlement in the dominions.

The 1920s were also years of mass unemployment, and the Communist Soviet Union was making inroads into the labor movement. After many wars, those on the homefront who had sacrificed for the war effort felt they deserved their just rewards.

In 1908, Henry Ford introduced the Model-T, in "any color you choose so long as it's black." In 1914, he opened his Highland Park, Michigan factory, equipped with the first electric conveyor belt assembly line. A Model-T could now be assembled in 93 minutes. Consequently, Ford had 45 percent of the new automobile market. He paid his workers the highest wages in the industry—a whopping five dollars a day. In return, he demanded that his workers live by his standards: wives were not to work or take in boarders, employees were not to drink in local bars, and families were to attend church each Sunday. He sent men out into the workers' neighborhoods to make sure his rules were being followed. Ford was considered a bigot and was also paranoid; he feared for his family's lives. By creating Greenfield Village near Detroit, he tried to recapture and reproduce what he viewed as a simple, happy past—the good old days.

Thus, science not only gave man a better knowledge of his world, and the technology to make living "easier," but it also gave him new means of destroying himself. The same gasoline engine used to propel automobiles and trains was reinvented for use in airplanes that could drop bombs—as early as World War I. Science and technology together began recreating industry, which for more people than Henry Ford meant bigger profits and anxieties.

Additionally, the advent of electrical lighting in both home and factory created shift work, which of course, interferes with established biological rhythms. Electricity also created a brighter night-life with more possibilities, and it gave the middle and upper classes new appliances to make living easier and more comfortable.

The assembly lines, with their shift work, forced workers to meet the demands of both man and machine. Workers could spend an entire shift in one place along the assembly line, repeating the same action again and again. Thus, a worker answered to two bosses—one human, one mechanical. Only one understood pain and fatigue, however, and only one could stop the other. Consequently, most workers were more likely to be driven by machines than to actually drive them.

This was the newly mechanized, scientific, controlled world which became the model for Huxley's *Brave New World*, which one critic regarded as "...an exercise in pessimistic prognostication, a terrifying Utopia."

In 1958, Huxley wrote *Brave New World Revisited*, in which he discussed what he perceived as the threats to humanity that had developed since the publication of his novel in 1932. These threats were overpopulation, propaganda, scientific advancement, and his belief that man must not give up his freedom for the unthinking ease of a life organized by the power of a few over the masses. This was something that had happened in Germany, Soviet Russia, and Communist China since 1932.

Huxley saw scientific progress as a vain deceit which would produce a world with no joy—one in which endeavors are frustrated and sexual satisfaction becomes ashes. *Brave New World* is the utopian nightmare of scientific deceit, unlike the futuristic novels of H. G. Wells, whose optimism held that man falls to rise again.

Master List of Characters

The Director—*In charge of the Central London Hatchery and Conditioning Centre. He has a secret to reveal.*

Henry Foster—*A Supervisor in the London Hatchery. He loves facts, figures, and statistics.*

Mustapha Mond—*The Resident Controller for Western Europe; one of ten Controllers in the World. He possesses some of the now forbidden books, like the Bible and the works of Shakespeare.*

Lenina Crowne—*A Beta Nurse in the Hatchery. She is well-conditioned to this New World—until she meets the Savage.*

Bernard Marx—*An Alpha-Plus expert in hypnopaedia who does not meet the physical standards of his group. He thus yearns for acceptance, which he hopes the Savage will grant him.*

Fanny Crowne—*A friend of Lenina, but not related. She works in the Bottling Room of the Hatchery and is well-conditioned.*

Benito Hoover—*An Alpha Worker at the Hatchery. He is an acceptor of conditioning and life as it exists and spends time with Lenina, which irritates Bernard.*

George Edzel—*Another Alpha Worker who is friendly with Lenina.*

Helmholtz Watson—*An Alpha-Plus lecturer and writer for the College of Emotional Engineering. His overly superior intelligence has alienated him from society in the same respect as Bernard's physical inferiority.*

The Warden—*An Alpha-Minus; in charge of the Savage Reservation.*

The Indian Guide—*He takes Lenina and Bernard into the Reservation.*

John the Savage—*Considered an outsider in his world of the Reservation. His mother Linda was from the Old World, thus rendering them both unacceptable.*

Linda—*John's mother. Left at the Reservation by the Director. She has aged as a normal human being and shocks the New World when she returns. She was a Beta Worker in the Hatchery.*

Popé—*He appears only in Linda and John's memories. He had been Linda's Indian lover and abuser. He supplied her with the alcohol she craved.*

Mitsima—*An Indian who tries to teach Indian skills to John.*

Dr. Shaw—*He supervises Linda's care when she returns from the Reservation, authorizing unlimited soma until her death.*

Human Element Manager—*He shows John the Electrical Equipment Corporation.*

Dr. Gaffney—*The Provost of the Upper School at Eton. He shows the Savage the school system.*

Miss Keate—*Head Mistress at Eton; she supervises the girls' training.*

Arch-Community-Songster of Canterbury—*Leads the Ford's Day Celebration. A special guest of Bernard's at the reception for the Savage.*

Nurse—*Attending nurse in Ward 81; she does not understand John's concern about Linda.*

Deputy Sub-Bursar—*He is called to distribute soma to the workers; he also calls Bernard about the Savage.*

Reporter—*A representative of The Hourly Radio who violates the Savage's seclusion. The Savage literally gives him the boot.*

Darwin Bonaparte—*Photographer for the feelies. Uses footage of the Savage at the lighthouse to create The Savage of Surrey feely.*

The following are members of Bernard's Solidarity Service group. They meet every Thursday to reinforce moral and cultural training:

Morgana Rothschild	Joanna Diesel	Tom Kawaguchi
Clara Deterding	Jim Brokanovsky	Fifi Bradlaugh
Sarojini Engels	Herbert Bakunin	The President

Summary of the Novel

Brave New World begins in the year A.F. (After Ford) 632, which is approximately the twenty-sixth century, in the Central London Hatchery and Conditioning Centre. The Director is taking a group of students through the Hatchery. As the Director is explaining the process of creating humans, the Resident Controller appears to finish the lesson.

Bernard Marx works in the Hatchery. He very much wants to have sex with Lenina Crowne, another worker in the Hatchery. Birth control has virtually been perfected, allowing everyone to be sexually free and totally available for anyone.

Lenina decides to accept Bernard's invitation to spend a week at the Savage Reservation in New Mexico. Her friend Fanny is not in favor of the idea because Bernard is so different from the other Alpha group members. Bernard himself feels alienated because his physical appearance is different from that of the other Alphas, and he often talks with Helmholtz Watson, another slightly alienated Alpha.

Bernard receives permission from the Director to visit the Reservation with Lenina. The Director remembers once visiting the place with his companion, from whom he became separated. Consequently, he returned from the Reservation alone.

At the Reservation, Bernard and Lenina are shocked by the primitive conditions. Bernard tries to remain scientific, while Lenina desires escape through *soma*, a drug that produces a dream-intoxicated state with no after- or side-effects. While watching Indian/Savage rituals, a semi-Indian creature approaches them, speaking in strange, ancient words. This is John the Savage.

John's mother, Linda, is from the Other Place, or the New World of Lenina and Bernard. She has grown old, fat, and quite ugly. She has used alcohol to replace the *soma* she once had. Bernard realizes that this must be the lost companion of the Director, then pregnant with his child, John. Bernard resolves to return John and Linda, which will both disgrace the Director and bring fame to Bernard. Bernard's plan works. The Director is humiliated and resigns. In this New World, children are generated in bottles and conditioned scientifically. Words like "mother," "father," and "family" are considered pornographic. Bernard exposes the New World to the Savage and becomes an instant celebrity with John, the freak everyone must meet. John finally refuses to meet any more people, and Bernard's pseudo-celebrity dissipates quickly. Helmholtz and Lenina attempt to understand this Savage John and his unorthodox ideals. John does move them somewhat, but all their years of conditioning cannot truly be overcome. Finally, everyone becomes embarrassed by John's grief when his mother dies, after falling into a *soma*-induced coma and failing to recognize him.

In order to preserve the stability of the community, Mustapha Mond must remove the irritants. Bernard is exiled to Iceland, and Helmholtz to the Falkland Islands. The Savage also wants to be exiled, but Mond refuses, choosing instead to continue social experiments with him. John takes over a lighthouse on the southern coast of England near Portsmouth. He desires solitude, preferring to be alone with his thoughts and memories. He resorts to various methods of self-flagellation to cleanse his soul. His hideaway is discovered and he again becomes the object of public curiosity, his privacy destroyed.

John takes what he sees as his only escape. He commits suicide.

Estimated Reading Time

The average reader should be able to complete *Brave New World* in approximately four to five hours. Once one becomes accustomed to a scientific vernacular and British spellings of some words, reading should progress smoothly.

The chapters of the novel can be grouped to aid the reader in understanding the progression of the plot. Chapters I through III introduce the themes of scientific advancement and technology through the Director's lecture to his students and the appearance of the Resident Controller Mustapha Mond. The rigidly controlled organization of the society is evident. Chapter III may cause some difficulty; the back-and-forth aspect of the scenes here is a complex, yet effective, literary device.

Chapters IV through VI advance the plot and begin to hint at some of the underlying tensions that exist in what the Director has portrayed as a perfect utopian world.

Chapters VII through X introduce John the Savage as the antagonist who will hold a mirror to this seeming utopian society and reveal its flaws. John's mother, Linda, has given him his preconceived ideas about her world.

Chapters XI through XV follow John's progression through and gradual rejection of the society his mother has told him is perfect. The imperfections of individuals in this world are also revealed.

Chapters XVI through XVIII carry the plot into the denouement of the last chapter with the philosophic debate between Mond and the Savage about the personal sacrifices that must be made to maintain a utopian society. The fates of the main characters are also decided.

Brave New World

Chapter I

New Characters:

The Director: *head of the Central London Hatchery and Conditioning Centre*

Henry Foster: *a worker at the Centre*

Lenina Crowne: *a nurse at the Hatchery*

Summary

The Director is escorting a group of new students through the Hatchery. He always wanted to give the initial educational tour himself. The students begin at the incubators, where human spermatozoa and ova are contained for the fertilization process. Each pair of sperm and egg will become either an Alpha- or a Beta-typed individual. Gamma, Delta, and Epsilon types undergo the Bokanovsky Process. This causes the fertilized egg to bud and create up to 96 identical individuals who will be trained to do identical jobs. The eggs are then imbedded in sow peritoneum (a pig's internal lining) and placed in large bottles. The bottles are placed on assembly lines, which move them along at a calculated rate. Thus, they reach the Decanting Room nine months, or 267 days, after fertilization, at a rate of eight meters a day.

Henry Foster supplies the statistical information to the students regarding the daily attention and conditioning each embryo receives with respect to how it will fulfill its predetermined social role. He convinces the Director to show the students to the Decanting Room, even though the afternoon is nearly over and time is running short.

Analysis

By having the Director explain the process of producing new human beings, Huxley has allowed the reader a unique perspective concerning the background and method of control in the New World. The motto "Community, Identity, Stability" states the goals of this controlled society.

The students trail the Director and they obediently write down his every utterance, which further demonstrates how orderly and controlled this system is. With obvious pompous pride, illustrating his sphere of influence and leadership, the Director personally takes charge of each new group of students.

In an era when most tenth-grade biology students have a working knowledge of in-vitro fertilization, the method described in the opening chapter may seem highly unscientific. However, in 1931, this was the stuff of science fiction: children created totally outside the womb, with no sense of parents or family. Control of population from birth is not a new idea; but the idea of prenatal population control, by shaping a fetus to a predestined social role, is something that perhaps only existed within the minds of scientists, fictional or otherwise.

Using the first five letters of the Greek alphabet to identify class and intelligence levels, Huxley allows the reader to deal with a classification system that has some sense of familiarity amidst the scientific blur.

The Bokanovsky Process for producing embryonic budding is obviously a point of pride with the Director. "You really know where you are. For the first time in history.... If we could Bokanovsky indefinitely, the whole problem would be solved...." is ironic. This is because identity, which once came from a sense of self, now comes from a feeling of oneness with no less than 95 other identical beings.

The date, A.F. 632, is not clarified yet, but the emphasis on the assembly-line production of people gives a clue to the meaning of the F. The practice of assembly-line production in factories was only

about 15 years old when this novel was written, but today's reader is so accustomed to assembly-line production that this point goes almost unrecalled. At the time of original publication, the assembly-line production of human beings was probably much more difficult a prospect to comprehend. Today, such a notion may not seem so far-fetched.

The official, sterile, statistical ease with which the Director and Henry Foster refer to human production and population control conjures up the image of a Detroit auto plant manager describing pick-up trucks. At one point, the Director casually compares the developing fetuses with developing film: as being tolerant only of red light.

Preconditioning fetuses for their futures saves training time later. That time may instead be used constructively for social conditioning and learning the pursuit of pleasure. Fetuses are totally conditioned to the job and climate for which they are destined. Necessary immunizations are completed before decanting to avoid any pain or other unnecessary discomforts.

The Director and Foster refer briefly to failures, although there is no reference as to whether these failures were destroyed. Thus, the suggestion of any type of abortion is altogether avoided, which is probably more than the reader of either 1932 or the present could accept. However, it seems safe to speculate that destruction of unacceptable specimens is probably an integral role of the assembly-line process.

The students, under the wings of the Director, are all male, and all of the primary Alpha characters in the novel are male as well. This illustrates a paternalistic society, with men making decisions and determining the destiny of the New World and its inhabitants.

Study Questions

1. What is the World State's motto?

2. Why is the Director leading the students through the Hatchery?

3. What is the year? When would this be, using our present dating system?

4. How are people classified?

5. What is the Bokanovsky Process?

6. How are the bottled embryos moved during their gestation periods?

7. Why are some females allowed a normal, sexual development? What percentage?

8. What had happened when the maturation process had been shortened?

9. How does the introduction of Henry Foster give a business-like feeling to the Hatchery procedure?

10. What does Lenina's reaction to the Director's familiarity show about their relationship?

Answers

1. The motto is "Community, Identity, Stability."

2. The Director always personally takes new students through the Hatchery because he is very proud of his position.

3. The year is A.F. 632; by using the date that Henry Ford opened the Highland Park, Michigan factory, the date is 2546 A.D.

4. People are classified using the first five letters of the Greek alphabet: Alpha, Beta, Gamma, Delta, and Epsilon. Alpha is the highest class.

5. The Bokanovsky Process causes the budding of one fertilized egg. Up to 96 identical humans can be produced. Only the lower classes receive the Process.

6. The bottled humans are moved eight meters a day for 267 days on an assembly line.

7. The Hatchery needs a supply of female ova (eggs) for the fertilization process. Thirty percent of the female embryos are thus allowed to mature.

8. When the maturation process was shortened, the individual was mentally and socially stuck at a childlike level, unable to perform simple adult tasks.

9. Henry Foster is like an accountant. He deals with facts and figures, rather than emotions.

10. Lenina does not seem bothered by the Director's advances. However, she does blush and her smile is referred to as deferential, which may mean submissive rather than agreeable.

Suggested Essay Topics

1. Describe the attitude of the Director toward his new students, and toward Henry Foster.

2. Compare the production of humans with the assembly-line process as it is used for products of the present time.

Chapter II

Summary

The Director continues leading the group of students through the Central London Hatchery. They have now moved from the Decanting Room into the Infant Conditioning Rooms. Uniformed nurses are setting out bowls of beautiful roses and stacks of books on the floor of one Conditioning Room. A group of khaki-clad, eight-month-old Delta infants is rolled in, stacked in compartments on industrial shelving. The babies are placed on the floor so they can see the roses and books. They happily begin crawling to the two fascinating objects, touching and playing with them. At a signal from the Director, the Head Nurse switches on loudspeakers that emit horrible shrieking sounds and alarm bells. The babies are terrified. Another lever is moved and the floor under the babies begins to send mild electrical shocks through their bodies. When the noise and shocks stop, the terrified crying of infants fills the room. When the Director has the nurses push the roses and books toward the infants, the crying becomes a howling. He orders the infants to be taken away.

Now that the students have observed a conditioning session, the Director patiently begins to explain the implications of what they have just seen. Deltas are not allowed to waste their time enjoying nonproductive things like nature or books. However, transportation to the country is to be consumed. So the lower classes are conditioned to love country sports, but to hate the beauty of the country. Thus they consume transportation and sports equipment, but do not linger since that would waste time. Since he has the undivided attention of the group, the Director decides to tell a story. There was once a little Polish boy named Reuben Rabinovitch who lived during the era of Our Ford. (Here, the Director dares to begin using what have become smutty four-letter words: mother, father, born. The students are embarrassed, but fascinated.) One night, Reuben's parents accidentally left the radio on in his room. The next morning, Reuben was able to repeat all that he had heard while he was asleep. This was the beginning of hypnopaedia (sleep-teaching). However, other experiments with children revealed that although the children knew facts, they could not relate any of their rote learning. Hypnopaedia was abandoned.

The Director then takes the students into a Sleep Conditioning Room. While facts that needed to be assimilated could not be taught through hypnopaedia, morals and social behavior could. Eighty children are napping. Small pillow speakers are whispering Elementary Class Consciousness for Betas. Each lesson is repeated 120 times, three times a week, for 30 months. Then a new lesson is begun. By the time each child is an adult, he/she has absorbed all the moral and social conditioning necessary to fit into the correct caste and proper place in society. The session ends when the Director becomes overly enthusiastic and accidentally awakens the children.

Analysis

In the 1920s, Ivan Pavlov (1849-1936) initiated the systematic study of conditioned responses and their implications for psychology. Classical conditioning is a learning situation that causes a response to a stimulus different from the usual or expected one. Pavlov performed the now well-known experiment with a dog. Dogs salivate when they smell food. He rang a bell each time he offered food to a dog. After a repetition of this pattern, Pavlov rang the bell but did not offer the food. The dog still salivated. This was

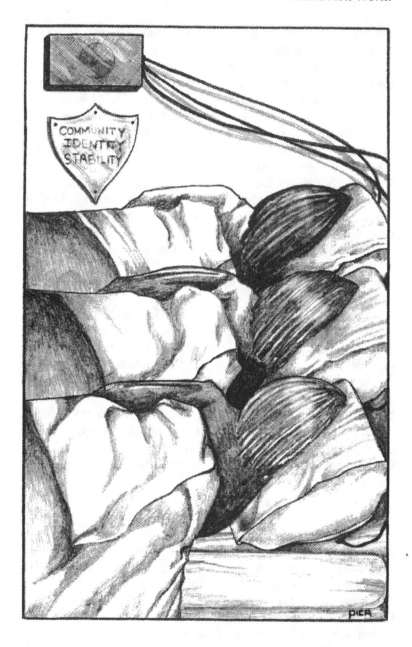

a conditioned response. The process can also be used for counter-conditioning to get rid of unwanted behavior. Pavlov's experiments became well-known and were often repeated to see what humans could learn or unlearn with conditioned response.

In 1958, Aldous Huxley wrote *Brave New World Revisited*. He states in Chapter 11:

Lacking the ability to impose genetic uniformity upon embryos, the rulers of tomorrow's over-populated and over-organized world will try to impose social and cultural uniformity upon adults and their children. To achieve this end, they will (unless prevented) make use of all the mind-manipulating techniques at their disposal and will not hesitate to reinforce these methods of non-rational persuasion by economic coercion and threats of physical violence.

Classical experiments have also shown that a process called extinction occurs when the conditioned stimulus (like the bell) was repeatedly presented without the unconditioned stimulus (the food). However, the conditioned response of fear seems to continue years after the initial incident, even without reinforcement. Childhood fears can last far into adulthood, when the person may have long forgotten the incident. Fear-producing events in adulthood can also linger, causing a conditioned response to which many war veterans can attest.

Another psychological term is discrimination. This means that a person can be trained to respond to a particular stimulus in one way and to a similar stimulus in another way. Using conditioning and discrimination, the Delta infants are trained to hate the non-productive beauty of the country, but still want to go to the country for sports and games. They have become the ideal consumers.

The fable of Reuben Rabinovitch is used by the Director to demonstrate the advances that have been made in the 600 years since Henry Ford. He can't resist some titillation of the students by using the words for family relationships that have now become smut. In a world where babies are decanted from bottles and raised in collective conditioning nurseries, family relationships and the words that describe them must be made things of derision. The accidental discovery of sleep-learning, its failure, and its abandonment reinforce the Director's moral to his fable: "You can't learn science unless you know what it's about."

Aldous Huxley includes an entire chapter on hypnopaedia in *Brave New World Revisited*. He writes, "Hypnopaedia, if it is effective, would be a tremendously powerful instrument in the hands of anyone in a position to impose suggestions upon a captive audience." He also states that children are much better subjects for this than adults, who have already formed social and moral patterns. Huxley cites studies that have been done in the 26 years since he wrote the novel. The unique individuality of humans keeps hypnopaedia from being effective in the same way all of the time. The genetic engineering and manipulation of the New World assures the necessary effect of this technique.

Study Questions

1. What is the age and social group of the infants being conditioned?

2. What is the first conditioning mechanism used? The second?

3. Why must the lower groups be conditioned to go to the country?

4. What words have become "dirty words"?

5. How is Reuben Rabinovitch able to repeat the G. B. Shaw lecture?

6. Why were early sleep-teaching experiments abandoned?

7. When was hypnopaedia first used successfully?

8. How often is each hypnopaedic lesson repeated to be successful?

9. The Director says that wordless conditioning is crude and wholesale. What reasons does he give for this?

10. Whose suggestions are incorporated into the children's minds?

Answers

1. The infants are eight-month-old, identical Delta Bokanovsky Group babies.

2. When the babies first touch the roses and books, alarm bells, sirens, and horrible noises scare them. Then the floor under them is electrified.

3. The lower groups are the larger percentage of the population and must be conditioned to go to the country to consume transportation and sports equipment.

4. Words like mother, father, born, parents, and any intimate family relationship words have become the "dirty words" in this New World.

5. A radio was accidentally left on in Reuben's room while he slept. The next morning he was able to repeat Shaw's speech word for word.

6. Sleep-teaching was abandoned because children could memorize facts that way but could not relate them as knowledge. They could only repeat by rote memory.

7. Hypnopaedia was first used successfully in A.F. 214, or about 2130 in contemporary time.

8. Each lesson is repeated 120 times, three times a week, for 30 months.

9. The Director says that wordless conditioning cannot make finer distinctions or instill complex behavior.

10. The Suggestions from the State are the ones that are instilled into all young minds.

Suggested Essay Topics

1. Why is it necessary, in A.F. 632, that words referring to family relationships have been made words of ridicule and pornography? How has this shaping of language been an aid to the conditioning process?

2. Hypnopaedia and/or hypnotic suggestion is used today to help people overcome problems (smoking, weight loss, self-esteem). Create a situation where someone who is open to suggestion receiving this type of treatment could be misdirected into deviant behavior.

Chapter III

New Characters:

Mustapha Mond: *the Resident Controller for Western Europe who joins the Director's group of students*

Fanny Crowne: *a co-worker of Lenina*

Bernard Marx: *an Alpha-Plus at the Conditioning Centre; he is attracted to Lenina. He is different from other Alphas and regarded as strange.*

Summary

Note: This chapter employs the device of quick scene cuts between the student group listening to Mond and the Changing Room of the Hatchery.

After taking the students through the Hatchery and early conditioning areas, the Director takes them outside to the supervised play areas. The children are all naked and playing in the sunshine. They are being encouraged in sports and erotic play. Continuing his lecture, the Director tells his students of the time when erotic play among children and adolescents was suppressed. Just as he is about to relate the problems this caused, Controller Mustapha Mond appears.

The scene then shifts to inside the Hatchery. It is four o'clock and time for the main day-shift to leave. Lenina Crowne is off-duty and ready to leave her station.

The story returns to the students, where Mustapha Mond has decided to talk to them himself. This is a great honor. He begins by discrediting all of history. He uses the words "mother" and "father," asking the students to try to imagine what it must have been like then. They are embarrassed.

Lenina Crowne goes into the locker room. She meets Fanny Crowne, a co-worker but no relation. (There are only 10,000 last names for the entire planet.) Lenina bathes and takes advantage of all the amenities of the bathing room.

The Controller is using the most vivid and, to the students, disgusting terms to describe family life in the Old World. After bathing, Lenina and Fanny talk. Fanny says that she has not been feeling well and has been advised to have a pregnancy substitute even though she is only 19. She shows Lenina the chemical hormones she has to take. Both are very matter-of-fact about the whole thing. Fanny is surprised that Lenina is still seeing Henry Foster.

Mond is continuing his litany about the past and the constraints of family and monogamy. He uses the names Ford and Freud interchangeably. Fanny reminds Lenina that four months with the same man would upset the Director. Long relationships are unacceptable. She advises Lenina to be more promiscuous, to have other men as well as Foster. Even though Fanny admits that she, like Lenina, doesn't always feel like going from man to man, they must conform to the social standards.

Mond reminds the students that they have been spared all the pain and suffering caused by pre-modern monogamy and family constraints.

In the men's dressing room, Henry Foster and a co-worker are casually discussing Lenina. The term "pneumatic" is used to describe anything wonderful or anyone who is sexually attractive and capable. Bernard Marx overhears the two and becomes infuriated at the way they refer to Lenina. He equates it to making her a piece of meat.

Fanny is shocked to hear Lenina talk about Bernard with interest. She has heard that he actually likes to be alone and she thinks his shorter-than-Alpha height means that something is wrong with him.

When Bernard hears Henry Foster mouth the adage, "Everyone belongs to everyone else," he calls Henry an idiot, because Bernard knows that this is a result of 62,400 sleep repetitions.

The scenes quickly click back and forth. Mond lists the terrors and destruction of the pre-modern world. Fanny and Lenina engage in girl-talk about men and clothes. Bernard becomes more upset as he listens in on Henry's discussion of women, especially Lenina, and sex. Intertwined with these three scenes are the sleep repetitions being done in the Conditioning Centre urging all toward Community, Identity, Stability, and consumptive consumerism.

At the end of the chapter, Controller Mond ends his lecture with a reference to *soma*. This is the hallucinogenic drug that is freely distributed to everyone in all castes. It provides everyone with the ability to escape unhappiness or distress by giving them a hallucination holiday with no after-effects. It keeps people from brooding—or thinking.

Analysis

This serves as a transition chapter from the background information delivered in the Director's and Controller's lectures into the plot of the novel. Because the reader needs the scientific data of the New World, the literary technique of virtually making the reader one of the students allows Huxley to explain the science he has created.

In Chapters I and II, the Director had related the hard facts of the creating and conditioning of life. The appearance of Mustapha Mond begins a philosophical look at the world. The interchanging of Ford and Freud, assembly-line science and psychology, show how the two have been used to create a perfectly controlled society. Mond's titillating use of words for family make pre-modern life a seething brew of monogamy, family, possessiveness, and selfishness leading to disease and destruction. Huxley's own satiric criticism of his time is carried through the words of Mond.

Since Lenina is a "freemartin," she has not been sterilized and is capable of reproducing. Keeping some of the population in this condition ensures that there will be fresh reproductive material available. The contraceptive belt that she wears is called a Malthusian belt, named after Thomas Malthus. In 1798, he wrote *Essay on Population*, in which he argued that a population tended to grow faster than its means of subsistence and should be controlled. At the same time Malthus was writing, Jeremy Bentham's aim to secure happiness for the greatest number of people by scientific legislation was circulating. Freemartin women are conditioned from childhood to use contraception. It is an open and acceptable part of a society that must be carefully controlled in population growth.

The parallel discussions of Lenina and Fanny, and Henry Foster and his co-worker are used to show the sexual freedom that is encouraged to eliminate the frustration and accompanying aberrations Huxley is criticizing in his own society. One needs to remember that this novel was written in 1932, when sexual permissiveness was much more frowned upon than it is in the 1990s.

Bernard Marx is different physically and mentally from his Alpha-Plus caste. Height is a physical statement of caste, but Bernard is short. His desire to be alone is also against the dictates of society. At this point in the novel, he seems to be the rebel: the one who may become the grain of sand in the grand machine.

The philosophical discussion being led by Mustapha Mond is a satire of the Sermon on the Mount. In fact, he refers to *soma* as having all the advantages of Christianity and alcohol with none of their defects: Ford and Freud joined to become God. Mond's statement, "Suffer little children," is a parody of Mark 10:14 from the New Testament, "Suffer the little children to come unto me...." as spoken by Jesus. In the Elizabethan English of the *King James Bible*, "suffer" meant to permit or to allow. Mond is welcoming the children to him as if he is their savior as well as their teacher.

Study Questions

1. What are the only new games the Controllers now approve? Why?

2. Who is the stranger who appears and startles the Director?

3. Why is Bernard Marx upset with Henry Foster's talk?

4. What has been advised for Fanny Crowne to relieve her depression?

5. What other name is Our Ford known by? When is this name used?

6. What does Controller Mustapha Mond talk about that shocks the students?

7. Why is Fanny worried about Lenina's dating habits?

8. Why is Bernard shunned by most people?

9. What is the purpose of Lenina's Malthusian belt? Why must she wear it?

10. What is *soma*?

Answers

1. Any new games must use more equipment than any other games that exist. People must consume manufactured goods.

2. The stranger is Mustapha Mond, the Resident Controller for Western Europe. He is one of ten Controllers for the entire world.

3. Henry's locker room talk about women, the feelies, and sexual activity—and his specific references to Lenina—upset Bernard.

4. Fanny has been advised to have a Pregnancy Substitute for three months. It should keep her healthy for three or four years.

5. Our Ford was also known as Our Freud when psychological matters were being discussed.

6. Mond makes numerous references to words like mother, father, nursing babies, families, and all words that have become smutty.

7. Fanny tells Lenina that she has been seeing Henry Foster exclusively for too long. She is even more shocked when Lenina shows interest in Bernard Marx. She advises Lenina to get out and sleep with more men.

8. Even though he is an Alpha-Plus, Bernard is shorter and more slightly built, not normal. He also enjoys being alone. Rumor says he had too much alcohol added to his blood surrogate when he was bottled.

9. Lenina's Malthusian belt contains a plentiful supply of contraceptives. Since she is a freemartin, she is capable of becoming pregnant, which would be the ultimate shame and disgrace.

10. *Soma* is a constantly available drug, which is euphoric, narcotic, and pleasantly hallucinogenic. People use it in their free time or in moments of stress to supply dream trips and to keep them happy always.

Suggested Essay Topics

1. Why does Mustapha Mond keep referring to the past premodern lives of families? Show how this is really a form of counter-conditioning and not just sensational.

2. Aldous Huxley uses the literary technique of moving across parallel scenes that change more quickly as the chapter progresses. Show how this technique allows examples of the pre-modern and modern world to be illustrated and how it also works as a device to move the novel from scientific explanation into plot movement.

3. Demonstrate how the intertwining of Ford and Freud blend the mechanical and psychological aspects of the New World.

Chapter IV

New Characters:

Benito Hoover: *an Alpha man who is friendly with Lenina*

George Edzel: *another Alpha man who is friendly with Lenina*

Helmholtz Watson: *an Alpha-Plus man who is almost too intelligent because he feels apart from and at odds with society; a friend and confidant of Bernard*

Summary

Part 1

The upper-class Alphas and Betas are coming from the locker rooms and heading for the elevators to the roof, where helicopters shuttle workers to home, games, or other entertainment. Lenina finds Bernard in the crowd. She tells him she wants to go to the Savage Reservation in New Mexico with him. Others around the

two are surprised and amused that Lenina wants to be with Bernard. He is embarrassed because of all the implications connected with Lenina's acceptance and that she is so public about it. The elevator operator is of the lowest caste, an Epsilon-Minus Semi-Moron. He has monkey-like features that brighten as he reaches the roof and sees the sun. As soon as he is ordered, he immediately and happily takes the elevator down. He has been bred for this simple repetitive job.

Bernard finds pure beauty in the blue sunlit sky. Lenina sees it only as a good medium for Obstacle Golf. She quickly flits off to join Henry Foster, leaving Bernard alone. Benito Hoover tries to be friendly and congratulates Bernard on his conquest. Bernard turns away, humiliated. Lenina and Henry speed off in his private helicopter to play Obstacle Golf. As she sees the lower castes going home from work, she voices her dislike of them and her happiness with her position, just as a well-conditioned Beta should.

Part 2

Bernard, still embarrassed and humiliated, makes his way to his own helicopter. As an Alpha, he does not have to use mass transit. He is unnecessarily sharp with the lower-caste attendants because he is always conscious of his below-average height, which he compensates with bravado. He flies to the Propaganda House to see Helmholtz Watson, who is the ultimate Alpha-Plus. The two men fly to Watson's building and go to his apartment to talk. They sit and discuss how different they feel from the society around them and how important words are, especially to Watson. Bernard suddenly feels that someone is listening at the door, but no one is there. Watson pities Bernard for his deep feelings of inadequacy, but keeps his thoughts to himself.

Analysis
Part 1

The transition to the plot of the novel is now complete. Part 1 of this chapter allows for more character development.

Lenina is a successful product of the conditioning process and truly believes that, "Everyone belongs to everyone else." She has

no concept of the emotional triangle she has created for Bernard because of her actions with Henry Foster. She does not understand the existence of jealousy and emotional pain because there is always *soma* to blank out those emotions.

Bernard's actions reinforce everyone's suspicions about mistakes made in his blood surrogate. His character development comes from what others say about him as well as from his own actions. He makes himself an outsider, but then uses that to feed his resentment over being that outsider.

The areas that Henry and Lenina fly over on their way to Obstacle Golf are real suburban areas of London that would be familiar to the English reader. Shepherd's Bush was an inner-city tenement and the others were middle-class suburbs. Stokes Peges was a small country town outside London. Futuristic fiction must give the reader some touches of his/her own reality to help imagine what might be from what is. Using London and, later in the novel, New Mexico locations gives the reader actual locations to which he/she may relate. Against these are Lenina's conditioned responses to seeing lower-caste individuals below her, literally and mentally.

Part 2

Bernard Marx's humiliation continues in his mind long after Lenina and the onlookers have left. He is even more harsh with the lower-caste workers. They always remind him of his inadequate height and build. He carries the mocking smiles and remarks of others as his own personal baggage. To compensate, he acts the bully. He tries to fit in and always feels alienated.

Likewise, the man whom Bernard feels is his soulmate, Helmholtz Watson, also feels the mental, if not the physical, alienation from society. Watson has all a man could want: physical superiority, any female he chooses, excellence in sports. Both men have a vague feeling that something is missing in their lives, even though they have all the best their world can offer. Watson compares words to x-rays that can go through anything. They are perhaps Romantics in the New World, searching for some kind of Truth and Beauty.

Study Questions

1. Where is Lenina when she tries to discuss the New Mexico trip with Bernard?

2. Why is Bernard embarrassed by Lenina's conversation?

3. What is the difference in the way Bernard and Lenina look at the warm blue sky when they reach the roof?

4. When Benito sees that Bernard is in a bad temper, what does he offer?

5. What does Lenina say during the flight with Henry that demonstrates she is a true product of conditioning?

6. How does Bernard treat those of lower caste than he? Why?

7. What caste is Helmholtz? What is his job?

8. What does Watson ask Bernard when the two men arrive at Watson's apartment?

9. What does Watson compare words to? Explain the comparison.

10. What does Watson quietly feel about his friend Bernard?

Answers

1. Lenina is in the lift (elevator) when she sees Bernard and openly talks about spending a week with him in New Mexico.

2. Bernard is always embarrassed by what he considers intimate conversations taking place in front of others.

3. Bernard remarks about the beauty of the sky. Lenina only sees it as a backdrop to play Obstacle Golf.

4. Benito offers Bernard *soma*. No one should be unhappy when the drug will bring instant contentment.

5. Lenina sees the colors of the lower castes. She repeats the conditioning phrases: "What a hideous color khaki is" and "I'm glad I'm not a Gamma."

6. Because Bernard is not as tall as an Alpha-Plus should be, he feels insecure around the lower castes. He is always sharp

and officious with those below him. He shouts at the lower-caste workers.

7. Helmholtz Watson is an Alpha-Plus. He is a lecturer on writing at the College of Emotional Engineering. He also writes various propaganda slogans and rhymes.

8. Watson asks Bernard if he ever feels that there is some sort of power inside him wanting to come out—something important to say.

9. Watson says that words are like x-rays and can pierce anything. However, he doesn't feel he's writing the words that can be x-rays.

10. Watson feels sorry for Bernard. He privately wishes that Bernard had more self-esteem and more pride.

Suggested Essay Topics

1. Explain the differences between Bernard's and Lenina's reactions to the sky when they are on the roof. From what you know of these characters so far, how do their differing views of the sky reflect their differing views of life?

2. Bernard overcompensates for his non-Alpha looks by being a bully with the lower castes. Why does he do this? Can you relate this to someone you know personally?

3. "Words can be like x-rays, if you use them properly—they'll go through anything." What does Helmholtz Watson mean? How has this statement often proven true in our own history? Is this why tyrants burn books?

Chapter V

New Characters:

The members of Bernard's Solidarity Service group: *Morgana Rothschild, Fifi Bradlaugh, Joanna Diesel, Clara Deterding, Tom Kawaguchi, Sarojini Engels, Jim Brokanovsky, and Herbert Bakunin*

The President of the Solidarity Service group

Summary

Part 1

Henry and Lenina have finished their rounds of Obstacle Golf and fly to their next entertainment. Below them is the artificial brilliance of the city, especially the Crematorium. Lenina wonders whether higher-caste bodies produce the same amount of by-products as lower-caste ones. Suddenly, she remembers waking up during a childhood hypnopaedic session and being frightened by the whispering before falling back to sleep.

Both Henry and Lenina take *soma* before going to the new nightclub across the street. Everything in the club is geared to inspire sexual activity and pleasure. When they return to Henry's apartment, they again take *soma* and prepare to go to bed together after Lenina has completed her conditioned contraceptive drill.

Part 2

Every other Thursday is Solidarity Service day for Bernard. After dinner with Watson, Bernard goes to the Fordson Community Singery. Nine of the required 12 group members are there when Bernard arrives. He immediately regrets taking the first available chair because Morgana Rothschild is seated on his left. He is embarrassed by her questions and has always had trouble talking to her because of her heavy black eyebrows that meet over her nose.

In fact, he finds something wrong with everyone in his assigned group as he looks at them seated around the circular table.

The President of the group begins by making the sign of the T and turning on the music synthesizer. The Solidarity Hymn is

played first. Special *soma* tablets are placed on the table and strawberry *soma* ice cream is handed around for each to drink. Twelve stanzas of the First Solidarity Hymn are sung, the cup is passed again, and the 12 stanzas of the Second Solidarity Hymn are sung. *Soma* begins to take its effect. The cup goes around a third time as Morgana begins to repeat the words of the ritual. This is followed by the Third Solidarity Hymn, as the *soma* and ritual begin to work the hypnotic magic on the 12. They begin to move and act as if some type of sacred revelation were about to happen, dancing, swaying, and shouting. Bernard joins in, but feels none of the evangelical sensations. A type of ritualistic line dance begins as the music becomes more primitive and sensual. The 12 pair off and six couples go to waiting couches for the ritualistic orgy that ends the group session.

On the top of the Singery, as they are waiting for helicopters, Fifi Branlaugh expresses to Bernard the joy and contentment she feels. He agrees for the sake of appearances, but inwardly he feels even more alone than before.

Analysis
Part 1

The community lives of Lenina and Bernard are described in this chapter. Lenina has thoroughly enjoyed her golf game with Henry and thus the two have become responsible consumers of travel, country, and sports equipment. During their return ride to London, it is not the beauty of the sunset that attracts them, but rather the artificial lights from the buildings.

This New World is just as segregated as the Old. Lower castes live in barracks divided from the homes of Alphas and Betas by a wall. Because of genetic engineering and psychological conditioning, no one questions the differences in accommodations. Dissatisfaction with one's place and discord between the "haves" and the "have-nots" does not exist; so there is no basis for class war or revolution. In 1917, 15 years before the publication of this novel, the world had witnessed the Russian Revolution combined with the horror of World War I. In the 1920s, England had high unemployment, strikes, overcrowding of the land, and the resulting social problems. Both England and the United States saw Communist influences behind the strikes and social unrest—the Red Scare. Some prominent writers and activists in both countries joined the Communist party, seeing its doctrines of communal sharing of wealth as the hope of the world. Fear of the have-nots rising up against the upper classes was prevalent, even with the devil-may-care attitude of the Roaring Twenties in the United States. These problems had been solved in Huxley's New World—but at a price.

Since birth is a scientific event, not an emotional one, so is death. The Crematorium is a factory like any other factory with the output of that factory, the recovered chemicals, being the most important thing. Lenina is not concerned by death because it too is only a scientific event with no emotional ties. Her only concern is whether upper and lower castes have the same chemical recovery rate. The Crematorium is a place of momentary fun when the helicopter rides the warm updraft. Since there are no emotional bonds formed during life, there is no sense of loss in death. As the pleasure of the evening continues, the main influences are sex and *soma*. As Lenina and Henry rush to the nightclub, the beauty of the night sky is something to be avoided and unnoticed. Free and natural beauty does not promote consumerism.

Part 2

Solidarity Service days are necessary to reinforce in the adult world what was instilled in the child—Community, Identity, Stability. The adulterated religious symbolism carries through the sessions. The sign of the T (for Ford's Model T) has replaced the sign of the cross. Solidarity Groups are made up of 12 people, the same number as the disciples of Jesus. The *soma* tablets and *soma* ice cream have replaced the bread and wine of the Christian communion ritual. All through the Solidarity Service a religious-like fervor is built up. Traditional church ritual has been blended with the more effusive practices of various evangelical groups. Hymns, chanting, and dancing all lead to the final culmination of sexual orgy instead of religious ecstasy. As scientific as this New World is,

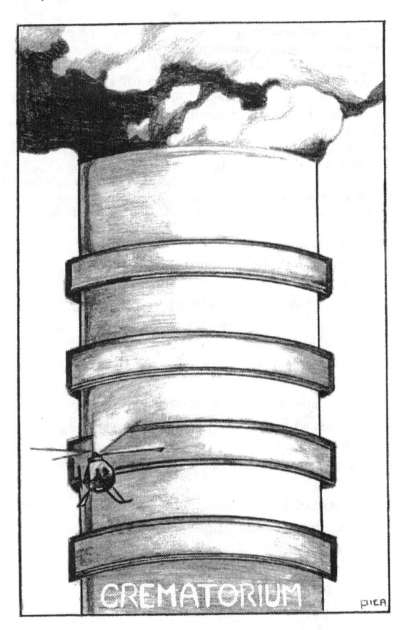

the deep-seated need for mystic belief still exists. This need has been guided into an evolution incorporating the conditioning necessary for its society. An emotional cleansing has taken place for everyone but Bernard. In 1844, Karl Marx had stated that "Religion...is the opiate of the people." *Soma* and sex have replaced religion, but it is still the "...opiate of the people"—that which subdues and controls them. Just as people through the ages have questioned and felt unfulfilled by religion, Bernard feels the same emptiness after his Solidarity Group session.

One interesting side note: Huxley has kept a traditionally English landmark—the clock nicknamed Big Ben. However, even this has been renamed in honor of Our Ford and is now Big Henry.

Study Questions

1. In what type of housing are the lower castes? How are Alphas and Betas housed?

2. What is done with the dead in the New World?

3. How does Lenina demonstrate that her childhood conditioning has been effective?

4. What does Lenina ask Henry about as she is getting ready to sleep with him?

5. When must Bernard attend his Solidarity meetings?

6. How many people are in each Solidarity Group? How are they seated?

7. Why is Bernard unhappy about sitting next to Morgana Rothschild?

8. What ritual is performed during the First Solidarity Hymn?

9. How does the Solidarity Group meeting end?

10. How does Bernard feel after the meeting?

Answers

1. The lower castes are housed in barracks, while the Alphas and Betas are on the other side of a wall in separate houses.

2. The dead are taken to the Crematorium where the bodies are burned and any valuable chemicals are recovered.

3. As Lenina flies over the lower-caste barracks, she repeats the conditioned phrases about other caste colors being ugly and how glad she is to be a Beta.

4. Lenina tells Henry how much Fanny admired her Malthusian belt and wonders where Henry bought it.

5. Bernard and everyone else must attend Solidarity Group meetings every other week. His day is Thursday.

6. There are 12 people in each Solidarity Group and they must sit man, woman, man, woman, around a circular table.

7. Morgana's heavy black eyebrows meet over her nose and this is very distasteful to Bernard.

8. During the First Solidarity Hymn, *soma* tablets and ice cream are passed from person to person.

9. Solidarity Group always ends with dancing, chanting, and the six men and six women pairing off for sex.

10. Bernard feels none of the contentment and release that Solidarity Group is supposed to provide.

Suggested Essay Topics

1. In the song "Bottle of Mine" that is performed by Calvin Stopes and his Sixteen Sexophones at the nightclub, what is the double reference with the word bottle and how does it apply to life in this New World?

2. Explain how the Solidarity Group meeting is designed to follow church ritual from various religions. Why do you think this was necessary?

Chapter VI

New Character:

The Warden: *an Alpha-Minus who is in charge of the Savage Reservation in New Mexico*

Summary

Part 1

Lenina begins to wonder if she has made the right decision in accepting Bernard's invitation to go with him to the Savage Reservation. She remembers the first time she met him, when all he wanted to do was be alone with her in the Lake District of England to walk and talk. When she does persuade him to fly to Amsterdam instead, he is surly with her friends and refuses to eat any *soma* ice cream. "I'd rather be myself," he said, "myself and nasty."

On the return trip over the English Channel, Bernard turns off the propeller to hover over the waves. He snaps off the radio Lenina has turned on. In an effort to control her terror, she begins spouting her conditioned phrases and urges him to take *soma* to get rid of his horrible mood. Satisfied with his actions, Bernard continues to London. Back in his apartment, Bernard weakens, takes *soma*, and beds Lenina.

When they meet the next day on the roof of the Hatchery, Lenina is happy and pleased as she joins Bernard in his plane. He is still upset by the way she refers to herself sexually and his own weakness the previous night. He says that people function as adults on the job but become pleasure-seeking infants everywhere else. Lenina doesn't understand any of what he is saying and thinks she is sexually unattractive to him.

Later, when Lenina is talking to Fanny, Fanny once again blames all on the rumored alcohol in Bernard's blood surrogate. Lenina still insists that she likes him, but acknowledges that he is odd.

Part 2

Bernard must see the Director to get permission to go to the Savage Reservation. His permit already has the signature of

Mustapha Mond and the stamp of the World Controller's Office; so there is not much the Director can do to keep Bernard from going. Almost unconsciously, he begins to remember his own trip to the Reservation 25 years ago and muses out loud. Bernard begins to feel very uncomfortable at this private moment. He senses that the Director does not want him to go and is about to reveal personal thoughts: that he is going to do the forbidden.

The Director also wanted to spend a week visiting the Savage Reservation. He took along a sexy Beta-Minus blonde girl with him. After eating a picnic lunch, they fell asleep in the afternoon heat. When the Director awoke, a thunderstorm began and the girl was gone. Searching for her proved fruitless and the search party the next day was unsuccessful. The assumption was that she had died. He admits that he sometimes still dreams about it. Bernard attempts some words of consolation.

Guilty with the realization of what he has just done, the Director bristles and becomes angry at Bernard to cover up his indiscretion. He reminds Bernard that some disturbing reports have come in about his behavior. Alphas are special and must make extra effort to conform to infantile pleasures. He warns Bernard that further reports could mean that he could be transferred to Iceland. He dismisses Bernard curtly.

Instead of being alarmed as he leaves the office, Bernard is almost elated. The Director had talked to him about personal matters. Later, he gloats over and embellishes the story as he talks to Helmholtz. Helmholtz has always been bothered by Bernard's boasting after events when he thought he came out the winner in a situation and then would swing into self-pity. Watson doesn't reply to Bernard's bragging or look at him. Bernard turns away, embarrassed.

Part 3

The Blue Pacific Rocket gets Bernard and Lenina to Santa Fe in six-and-a-half hours. Their hotel is excellent and has all the New World synthetic amenities. Lenina is pleased, while Bernard is resigned and warns her that the Reservation will be much less accommodating. She still says she wants to go.

The Warden begins his set introductory speech. Distractedly, Bernard remembers he left the cologne tap on in his London rooms and that he must call Watson to turn it off before it costs a fortune. He pays little attention to the droning on by the Warden. Lenina has taken *soma* and is really not connecting with anything the Warden says. She doesn't even blush when he leeringly mentions that children are born on the Reservation. When Bernard finally contacts Watson, Watson has some disturbing news. Bernard is to be sent to Iceland. Instead of being bothered by this news, Bernard is puffed up with his own self-importance in receiving such attention, but then be becomes angry at the Director. Finally, Lenina talks him into *soma* complacence.

Word is sent that the plane is ready to take Bernard and Lenina on an air tour of the area and they land by lunch time at the valley of Malpais. Bleached bones line the inside to the electrified fence where animals have run into it. The pilot thinks this is funny and Bernard laughs too, then falls into a *soma* sleep, missing the spectacular southwestern landscape. At Malpais, the pilot tells them that the Savages are staging a dance that afternoon at the pueblo and that a guide will take them there. He assures them that he will return tomorrow to pick them up and assures Lenina that the Savages are tame, but very funny.

Analysis
Part 1

Lenina is fascinated, yet somewhat repelled, by the oddity of Bernard's behavior. She is incapable of understanding his desire to be alone, to talk, to refuse the bliss of *soma* sometimes. His actions over the Channel and his talk about freedom scare her because this is all against her well-conditioned view of life with *soma* and happiness. Bernard's bravado and facade begin to show cracks when he finally does take so much *soma* that he falls into a stupor after he beds Lenina. As usual, she doubts her sexual attraction; yet she is drawn to Bernard still. One begins to wonder: who will change whom, and how much of Bernard's rebelliousness is a pose?

Part 2

The scene in the Director's office is a foreshadowing that perhaps all is not perfect in this most perfect world. Bernard likes to think he has rid himself of his hypnopaedic conditioning, but the Director's frankness bothers him. The Director's story about his experience at the Reservation belies the calm, unruffled exterior he displayed with the students in the first two chapters, as does the fact that he still dreams about the woman he left. His officious, haughty attitude with Bernard after his revelation mimics Bernard's attitude with others when he thinks he has been slighted. However, since the Director has more clout, he can make good on his threat of exile.

Instead of feeling beaten, Bernard feels strangely excited that he could arouse such feelings in someone of authority. As usual, he swings between aggrandizement and self-deprecation. He is the braggart with Helmholtz, but then blushes and turns away, unable to keep up appearances. Helmholtz was right: words are like x-rays, but Bernard has pierced himself.

Part 3

With Lenina at the Reservation resort area, he has become his officious self again, carefully warning her about the primitive accommodations, almost as if he's saying to her, "I can take it, but I'm not sure if you can." He doesn't feel he needs the Warden's information and he becomes distracted by the fact that he left the cologne tap on in his flat, a petty thing to remember considering the importance of his trip. He thinks of nothing else but calling Helmholtz concerning the tap. While Lenina escapes her boredom and lack of understanding in her typical fashion (*soma*), Bernard can only focus on a trivial thing back home when he should be totally absorbed with what he thought he wanted—a visit to the Savage Reservation. Actually, he wants to use this trip as a way to make himself look more important when he returns home, as something to feed his ego. The Director had to let him go to the Reservation and Lenina Crowne wanted to accompany him.

Bernard's indignation with the Director's action on the Iceland transfer sows the seeds of revenge and becomes a part of the basis for his actions against the Director, including using John and Linda in later chapters. Certainly, his own actions could not be at fault. Following his usual pattern, he turns his deep-seated feelings of rejection and inadequacy on someone else. He binges on *soma* and sinks into sleep, totally oblivious to the beauties of nature that he professes to seek. Lord Byron, one of the major Romantic poets, portrayed himself as a grand hero who was buffeted by the constraints of his society, creating his own martyrdom. This is Bernard's grandiose view of himself. Bernard is not the romantic Byronic hero he imagines himself to be.

As he did with London, Huxley uses real place names from the Southwest of the United States to give the reader a frame of reference. The name he chooses for the valley where the pueblo is located is Malpais, which is Spanish for bad country or bad land.

Study Questions

1. To what does Henry Foster compare Bernard?

2. What does Bernard want Lenina to do on their first afternoon together?

3. When Bernard and Lenina meet her friends in Amsterdam, how does he behave?

4. How does Bernard frighten Lenina during their return over the Channel?

5. What is the Director's attitude toward Bernard's trip to the Reservation?

6. What does the Director sometimes dream about regarding his experience at the Reservation?

7. How does the Director threaten Bernard for his reported behavior?

8. What are Bernard's only thoughts during the Warden's lecture?

9. How does Bernard react when he hears the Director has made good on his threat of exile?

10. How does the Gamma pilot refer to the Savages and the Reservation? What word does he keep using?

Answers

1. Foster calls Bernard a rhinoceros who has not been affected by conditioning.

2. Bernard wants to take Lenina to the Lake District to walk and talk alone.

3. Bernard sits at the ice cream bar and sulks, refusing to take *soma* or enjoy himself in any way.

4. Bernard frightens Lenina by dropping very close to the dark waves of the Channel and turning off the engine to hover quietly above them.

5. The Director does not want to give his permission for Bernard's trip, but he cannot go against Mustapha Mond's signature.

6. The Director sometimes dreams about not being able to find the girl he took to the Reservation, and the search in the thunderstorm.

7. The Director says that if any more reports come in Bernard will be exiled to Iceland.

8. All Bernard can think about is calling Helmholtz to have him turn off the cologne tap in Bernard's flat because it will be so expensive.

9. Bernard is outraged that this could be done to him. Then he begins to think of a way to get his revenge.

10. The Gamma pilot refers to everything on the Reservation as funny, whether it is the dead animals along the fence or the Savages. He says the Savages are tame but funny.

Suggested Essay Topics

1. Bernard rationalizes the Director's actions toward him. How does he turn his own feelings of inadequacy into anger against the Director? How does he blame the Director for his own mistakes?

2. Why do you think Lenina is drawn to Bernard, even though she calls him so very odd?

3. Is Bernard's action over the Channel: (a) to truly enjoy the night sea, (b) to deliberately frighten Lenina, and/or (c) to punish Lenina for making him take her to Amsterdam and socialize? Explain your choice.

Chapter VII

New Characters:

John: *the strange blonde-haired, blue-eyed Indian who speaks to Bernard and Lenina*

Linda: *John's mother and an outcast of the pueblo; she too is white*

The Indians of the pueblo

Summary

Bernard and Lenina stand below the mesa looking at the pueblo of Malpais. She feels uneasy in this place with the Indian guide. Drums begin a heartbeat-like rhythm as they walk and then climb to the top of the mesa. The Indians' dark brown bodies are painted and decorated with feathers, silver, bone, and turquoise and their smell becomes stronger. Some carry snakes. Lenina is repulsed by the smell of humanity and the dirt. She sees an old Indian and is unable to comprehend his aged, wrinkled body. Bernard takes on the attitude of a professor and explains that the technology of the New World prevents all diseases and effects of aging, at least until the age of 60; then people just die. Lenina discovers she has forgotten her *soma* and Bernard has none. She must experience what is to come on her own. Since his morning *soma* has worn off, Bernard feels he must appear in control. He keeps remarking about life on the Reservation and mothers giving birth to babies.

As the Indian guide leads them on through the pueblo, they see the sick and elderly, rubbish and dirt. They are led down a ladder through a long odor-filled room and into the sunlit terrace where the drums are beating. The rhythm momentarily entrances Lenina because it reminds her of the synthetic rhythm used during the Solidarity Group Service. She is carried away by the sound, then harshly pulled back by the appearance of the costumed dancers. Onlookers begin to shout and chant as the dance leader tosses a snake into the crowd. An old man emerges from an underground opening, followed by symbols of an eagle and a crucifix, and an 18-year-old boy in a breech cloth. He moves among the dancers in a trance. An Indian in a coyote mask raises a whip and lashes the boy repeatedly across his back. Lenina screams. The old man touches a white feather to the boy's bloody wounds and shakes blood three times over the snakes. The drums beat wildly and the people disperse. Three old women appear to carry the unconscious boy away while Lenina sobs. Then all is gone; Bernard and Lenina are alone.

The sound of footsteps comes toward them from behind. Bernard turns to see a young man in Indian dress, but with blonde braids and blue eyes. He speaks to them in a peculiar English that has a Shakespearean overtone. The blonde Indian expresses regret over not being allowed to be the sacrifice. The ritual brings the rain and makes the corn grow. He talks of Pookong and Jesus, but then is quiet as he sees the young, white beauty of Lenina. Bernard barrages him with questions. His mother is Linda and she is from the Other Place. His father's name was Thomakin and had left before he was born.

Linda's house is separated from the rest of the village, but it is just as squalid and smelly. A fat blonde woman dressed as an Indian opens the door. She is tanned, with dry wrinkled skin, and is missing some teeth. She grabs Lenina and hugs her in a slobbering, smelly embrace, recognizing her as a person from the Other Place. She begins a rambling litany about her horrible existence, the shame of giving birth, her terrible life on the Reservation, and her memories of her former life. She had been a Beta in the Fertilizing Room. Her contraception had failed and there was no Abortion Centre here on the Reservation. She named her son John and lived as an outcast in the Indian society because of her New World ideas. Had she been able to return, she would have been an outcast in the Other Place also because she had given birth. Her outrageous actions have stigmatized John also. She had tried to condition him, but didn't know enough to do it correctly. She can't stop talking to the two people she thinks should understand her.

Analysis

Huxley uses this chapter to introduce John the Savage, who will become the antagonist in the novel. The character of Linda provides an ironic ending to the story of the Director's trip in Chapter VI, Part 2. There are also vivid descriptions of the setting, both manmade and natural, and the Savages who inhabit Malpais. The description of the sacrificial ceremony and dance is deliberately long and involved to fill the reader's mind and senses and to make him/her a witness to the spectacle along with Bernard and Lenina. Huxley is obsessed with stench and filth and this is interwoven with the ceremony. This literary color is one of the hallmarks of Huxley's writing. He juxtaposes the natural stark beauty of the southwestern United States with the primitive conditions of the pueblo.

John's sudden appearance and his strange speech surprises and then excites Bernard. As he questions this strange blonde creature, he realizes that here is his means to get his revenge on the Director. Now he must complete the circle and meet the woman.

The 25 years of agony and shame that come tumbling from Linda reveal that New-World contraception is not perfect and abortion is totally acceptable. Huxley again uses his obsession with stench when Linda's odor reminds Lenina of the blood surrogate used for embryos.

The heartbeat rhythm of the drums pulls at Lenina with the same orgiastic power of the Solidarity Service, showing that the New World has recognized the need to tap into the deepest primitive human emotion, but to dress it up in a New World veneer. The symbols of the Indian dance are a strange combination of pagan and Christian, just as the New World has used the sign of the T to combine religion with technology. The whipping of the boy is much like the scourging of Jesus before the crucifixion. Three women remove his unconscious body, just as three women came to prepare the body of Jesus, and three dark queens took away the mortally wounded body of King Arthur.

Cracks are appearing in the facade of the New World as well as within its individual members.

Study Questions

1. Why doesn't Lenina like the Indian guide?

2. To what does Lenina compare the top of the mesa?

3. What shocks Lenina about the old man?

4. How does Bernard try to appear strong and brave?

5. Of what do the drums remind Lenina?

6. How does the new Savage appear different?

7. What about Lenina fascinates the blonde Indian?

8. Why is Bernard so excited with the answers the Savage gives to his questions?

9. Why was Linda segregated and shunned by the rest of the pueblo?

10. What can the reader infer Linda hopes will happen now?

Answers

1. The Indian guide says nothing and smells bad.

2. The top of the mesa reminds Lenina of the view from the Charing T Tower.

3. The old man is wrinkled and sagging. Lenina has never seen the real signs of aging.

4. Bernard talks about mothers, babies, and birth. He tries to act very urbane about what he sees.

5. The drumbeat reminds Lenina of the rhythms used during the Solidarity Services, especially the orgy ending.

6. The new Savage has blonde hair and blue eyes. He speaks to them, but his manner of speech is strange.

7. Lenina is dressed differently; she is fair-skinned, clean, and beautiful.

8. Bernard begins to realize that this is the Director's child and a means to Bernard's revenge.

9. Linda misused the Indian drugs and was openly promiscuous.

10. Linda sees Bernard and Lenina as her salvation because they will take her back to the Other Place where she belongs.

Suggested Essay Topics

1. How is the whipping of the boy and the ceremony of sacrifice a blending of Christian and pagan rites into a new mythology?

2. Imagine you are Lenina listening to Linda ramble on. What is going through your mind? What are your emotions?

Chapter VIII

New Characters:

Popé: *Linda's Indian lover*

Mitsima: *John's Indian mentor*

Summary

While Linda cries and raves inside the isolated house, Bernard and John walk and talk outside. John says he can remember no other life but here on the Reservation. He remembers a time when he was a boy and he and Linda were lying on the same bed for their siesta. He was awakened by the sound of a man and his mother's laugh. He doesn't understand the man's words, but hears his mother's, "No." The man grabbed his arm, yanked him from the bed, put him in the other room, and closed the door. The young John screamed and cried, but no answer came from the other room.

This memory fades to another. He and Linda are with the other women weaving blankets. He was playing with the other children in a corner of the loom room. Suddenly, the women began yelling at Linda and pushed her from the room. They hate her and she doesn't understand them. Linda's Indian lover Popé was waiting at their house with mescal. They both became drunk and fell asleep, leaving John alone. Another afternoon, the village women came into the house, held Linda on the bed, and began whipping her. John tried, but could not stop them. His mother could not understand why she cannot freely have sex with any man she wants. She takes out her rage and hurt on John when he calls her mother.

Throughout his childhood, John heard stories of the Other Place and the Indian men tell him their lore. In his mind, the two mythologies fuse into a personal set of beliefs. Linda became more of an outcast because of her promiscuity, and John along with her. She did teach him to read and write. The only book she had was one on embryo engineering, which she did not fully understand. Reading became John's escape from the cruel jibes of the other boys. Finally, his reading took him beyond Linda's ability to explain. The old men gave him answers from Indian lore and John blended these, also.

In one of his rare moments of generosity toward John, Popé brought him an ancient copy of Shakespeare that he found. For John, this opened up a whole new world. The more John read from the thousand-year-old plays, the more his hatred of Popé grew. One night, the words of Hamlet (about the relationship between Polonius and Gertrude) came to his lips as he tried to stab Popé while he lay with Linda. Instead of hitting him, Popé just laughed and chased him away.

John's memories move forward to when he was 15. Mitsima was not able to teach John to work clay. He showed John shapes of nature and clay rope water pots. As they worked, John sang songs of the Other Place that Linda had taught him, and Mitsima sang native songs and chants. At 16, John watched the girl he loved marry someone else. He was not good enough for any of the Indian girls. Later that year was the time of initiation for the boys of the tribe who would move into manhood. As the boys climbed down into the Antelope Kiva, John was pulled out of line. He was denied the initiation. He walked out onto the mesa alone and, by the light of the full moon, performed his own blood initiation ritual.

The word "alone" touches a part of Bernard and he admits that he also feels alone, which surprises John. Linda had told him that no one was ever alone in the Other Place. John tells about having

to go to the mountain by himself to dream of his sacred animal. He pretended he had been crucified, but succeeded only in fainting and cutting his head. Bernard cannot look at the scar. He now feels sure who John's father is and wants to take John back to London. At John's request, Linda will return also. At first Bernard is hesitant about her, but he then realizes how much more perfect his revenge on the Director will be with Linda. Naively, John is elated at going to the place Linda has painted as an Eden. He quotes Miranda from *The Tempest* by William Shakespeare, "O brave new world that has such people in it."

Analysis

Bernard's discussion with John confirms Bernard's suspicions about the Director, and ties in with the Director's comments on his visit to the Reservation. Bernard now knows he has the means for his revenge and thus, a way to bring the Director down and add to his own self-importance.

John's memories of times in his life when he was made the scapegoat for the hate against his mother and was shunned by the tribe also stir similar feelings of alienation in Bernard. One difference is that John has been a true innocent victim, while Bernard is a victim of his own feelings of inadequacy. The two of them exist as outsiders in their respective societies and Bernard perceives this as a bond between them. In spite of the fact that Linda is considered the whore of the pueblo and John her bastard son, his love for her and his interest in her talk of the Other Place remain constant. He doesn't see the disgust Lenina has for Linda or Bernard's shudder at his scar. He has been Linda's protector and defender, even though she has mistreated and neglected him and has often been in a drunken stupor. He immediately includes her when Bernard offers to take him to London. Escape without her doesn't even cross his mind.

John's reference to Miranda and his quotes are from Shakespeare's *The Tempest*. Miranda has been stranded on an island for twelve years with only her exiled and bitter father Prospero and his deformed slave Caliban. Duke Prospero uses magic to shipwreck his persecutors on the island and plans to punish them.

When Miranda sees these new people she remarks:

> O, wonder!/How many goodly creatures are
> there here!/How beauteous mankind is! O brave
> new world,/That has such people in't!
> (V.i. 180-183)

Shakespeare's use of "brave" means handsome and noble, not courageous. Just as Miranda has no experience with other people and their deceitfulness, so John believes the New World, or the Other Place, will be the perfect world Linda has described, where he will finally escape the hurt and prejudice of the Reservation. This New World will be brave in Shakespeare's meaning, without the dirt, old age, and disease he has witnessed during his life. A foreshadowing of possible problems to come are in Bernard's final words: "And, anyhow, hadn't you better wait till you actually see the New World?"

Study Questions

1. What is one of John's earliest memories?
2. What do the women do to Linda in the weaving room? Why?
3. How do the women punish Linda for her promiscuity?
4. When John calls Linda "Mother," what does she do? What does he always call her after that?
5. Why does John often turn to the old men of the tribe?
6. Why is John always in ragged clothes? What is his solace?
7. What book does Popé bring for John?
8. What does Mitsima teach John?
9. What does John do when he is denied the initiation rite?
10. When Bernard offers to take John to London, what does John ask?

Answers

1. John remembers being locked out of Linda's room so Popé could have sex with her.

2. Linda had broken some threads on the loom. The women scream at her and chase her out.

3. The women of the pueblo break into Linda's house, hold Linda down on the bed, and beat her.

4. Linda slaps John when he calls her Mother. After that, he always calls her Linda.

5. The old men of the tribe can use tribal lore to explain many things to John that are beyond Linda's comprehension.

6. Linda has no idea how to mend or wash clothes; so John always looks ragged and dirty. He uses his reading as his escape.

7. Popé had found an ancient copy of Shakespeare's plays in a trunk. He brings the book to John.

8. Mitsima is kind to John. He tries to teach him how to make decorative and practical pottery and promises to teach him how to make a bow.

9. John goes to the edge of the mesa and sits facing the moon. From his own mixed-up mythology, he creates his own initiation rite.

10. John wants Linda to go to London, too.

Suggested Essay Topics

1. Discuss John's affection for and defense of Linda, despite the fact of her abuse and neglect of him and her continual drunkenness.

2. How does John blend Linda's stories and the tribal mythology to create his own religion? Why does he feel he must have his own initiation?

3. Compare Miranda's speech as quoted in the Analysis with John's use of her words. What kind of world does each imagine?

Chapter IX

Summary

Lenina immediately retreats into an 18-hour *soma* holiday when she returns to the guest house, while Bernard lies awake and makes plans. In the morning, he goes to Santa Fe to call Mustapha Mond. Mond agrees that John and Linda should be brought to London and arranges all the necessary paperwork. When Bernard returns to the Reservation, he treats the Warden with his typical officious disdain while orders from Mond are put into action.

John comes to the rest house seeking Bernard during the time he is gone. When there is no answer, he sits and cries, thinking he has been deserted. Then he goes to look in the window and sees Lenina's green suitcase. He picks up a rock and breaks the window. Once inside, he opens the suitcase and lovingly handles her things and breathes in her perfume. He whispers her name, then hears a sound from the other room. As he looks into the bedroom, he sees Lenina lost in her *soma* dreams, and kneels by her bed. Lines from *Romeo and Juliet* fill his head. Thoughts of unzipping her pajamas go through his mind and he is ashamed. He hears the sound of Bernard's returning plane and runs from the guest house to meet the man he thinks is his savior.

Analysis

This chapter serves to link John's life on the Reservation to his life as it will be in the Other Place, his dream of Eden. His adoration of Lenina becomes apparent. He has been beaten, neglected, and ostracized. His whole life has been one of dirt, disease, and aging. His one love was married to someone else. Lenina is his fantasy come-to-life, a fantasy he has created from the plays of Shakespeare. When John thinks of Linda with Popé, the words of Hamlet in reference to his mother come to mind, while looking at Lenina brings Romeo's words about Juliet to his lips. He sees her as representing all the purity in the world. Just as Miranda in *The Tempest* is too naive and unworldly to see the true nature of her visitors, John adores what he thinks Lenina must be. He does not realize that she is what his mother once was and that her way of life is exactly what caused all of Linda's problems on the

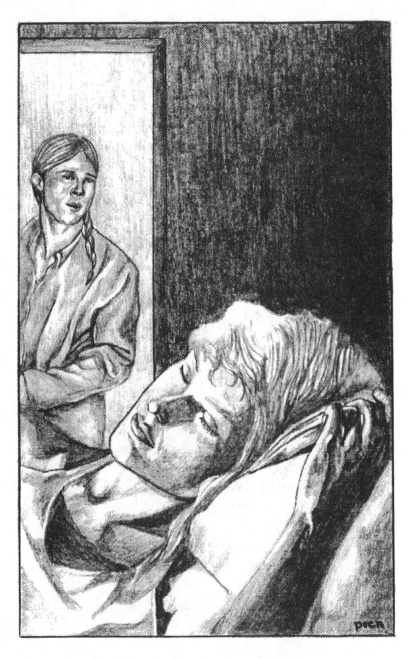

Reservation. The height of John's ideal will parallel the depth of his disillusionment. He has put Lenina and her world on such a pedestal, because of Linda's mythic stories, that the ironic realization of that world will crash in on him.

Study Questions

1. How does Lenina handle the disgust of her visit to the Reservation when she returns to the guest house?

2. Does Bernard sleep? Why?

3. Whom does Bernard call from Santa Fe? Why?

4. What does Mond do when he receives Bernard's call?

5. Why does Bernard treat the Warden the way he does?

6. How does John feel when he comes to the rest house?

7. Why does John break the window?

8. How does John handle Lenina's clothes and make-up?

9. Does John touch the sleeping Lenina? Why?

10. What causes John to leave?

Answers

1. Lenina takes enough *soma* to sleep for 18 hours.

2. Bernard lies awake planning John's trip.

3. Bernard calls Mustapha Mond directly to get permission for John and Linda to come to London.

4. Mond immediately sends permission for Bernard to take John and Linda off the Reservation.

5. Bernard feels very self-satisfied with his call to Mond and he has to flaunt his importance.

6. John thinks that he has been deserted and Bernard will not take him to London. He sits and cries.

7. John sees Lenina's green suitcase and he must get in the room to touch something that is hers.

8. John handles Lenina's things as if he were touching the relics of a saint.

9. John kneels at Lenina's bed but feels he is unworthy to touch her.

10. John hears Bernard's plane and runs out to greet him.

Suggested Essay Topics

1. Explain why you think Bernard called Mond directly, and what the plan is that he devised during his sleepless night.

2. Detail how Linda's stories of her world have created the fantasy that causes John's adoration of Lenina.

Chapter X

Summary

It is 2:27 p.m. at the Central Hatchery and all is proceeding as it should in embryo development and conditioning. However, a grave and worried Director enters the Fertilizing Room with Henry Foster. They are discussing someone who wants to meet with the Director. The meeting has been set in the room that has the largest number of high-caste workers to make an example of the person who is coming. Foster comments that one person is no real loss because another can always be made. Society is what is important.

When Bernard enters the Fertilizing Room he is a bit too bold, then backs off. The Director asks that all the workers stop what they are doing and listen. He then launches into a diatribe itemizing examples of Bernard's unorthodox behavior, ending by turning to him and asking if there is any reason why sentence should not now be pronounced. Now is Bernard's chance. He returns to the door and opens it to reveal John and Linda.

As a bloated, aged Linda waddles into the room, a gasp of horror moves through the workers. When she sees the Director "Thomakin," she moves toward him, asking if he remembers her.

Finally she hollers his name and engulfs him in her huge arms, hurling the final insult, "You made me have a baby." She then uses the word "mother." The room becomes silent; the Director is pale and shaken. Then John is called. He runs into the room and falls on his knees saying, "My father." Hysterical laughter rolls through the room. The humiliated Director runs from the room as the laughter swells to a crescendo.

Analysis

"This is a hive of industry." The Director's metaphor is more true than he realizes. All social insects exist in a strictly regulated society, each ant, bee, or termite living out its life while dutifully performing its job as predestined from the moment the queen lays the egg in its cell, each knowing its place. Any anomaly is destroyed because it is a threat to the existence of the whole. Huxley extends his metaphor through the next several paragraphs to emphasize his point. The Director sees Bernard as the anomaly in his hive and plans a public demonstration of what happens to those who disturb the harmony of the hive/society.

Bernard enters, puffed up with his own importance, which fades a bit under the Director's gaze. The Director's accusation of Bernard is designed to bring public humiliation and ensure that everyone else witnesses what happens when, "The security and stability of Society are in danger." It also echoes the public condemnations that were used in the then 15-year-old Soviet Union of Huxley's day. Bernard's last name, Marx, is a reminder of Karl Marx, whose social theories stunned and frightened the Anglo-European world less than a century earlier.

Instead, it is Bernard who humiliates the Director with the entrance of Linda and John. Linda's confrontation of "Thomakin" and her flinging of the words "have a baby" and "I was its mother" cause a complete silence in the room. The paternalistic, chauvinistic attitude still exists in this New World for John's "My father" causes derisive laughter instead of shocked silence. The smuttiest words are still reserved for women. The Director's world has crumbled in a very few minutes, more in derision than in obscenity.

It is also a touch of irony that the Director meets Linda in the Fertilizing Room, the same room where she worked when they met, and since it was his fertilization of her that caused the whole situation.

This is the total reversal of fortune for the Director who was presented in Chapters I and II as a man in control of his own destiny and a complete product of his society. In a matter of minutes, his life has become a matter for derision and scorn.

Study Questions

1. To what does the Director compare the Bloomsbury Centre?

2. Why does the Director choose the Fertilizing Room to meet Bernard?

3. Why is it important that high-caste workers are witnesses?

4. How does Bernard begin the meeting?

5. Of what does the Director accuse Bernard?

6. What is to be Bernard's punishment?

7. How does Linda try to act toward the Director?

8. What is the reaction in the room to Linda's revelation?

9. What is the reaction to John's calling the Director his father?

10. How does the Director leave?

Answers

1. The Director calls the Centre a hive of industry.

2. The Director plans to make a public example of Bernard in front of high-caste workers.

3. High-caste workers are the most intelligent and the most capable of rebellious thoughts. This will be a lesson for them.

4. Bernard is self-important and self-confident, but nervous. He speaks too loudly at first.

5. Bernard is accused of heretical views on sport and *soma*, having an unorthodox sex life, and refusing to obey Our Ford.

6. Bernard will be dismissed from his post and sent to the lowest Sub-Centre on Iceland.

7. Linda tries to be the sexy, seductive woman she once was, but is actually a parody of what she once was.

8. An uncomfortable, embarrassed hush falls over the room.

9. Everyone in the room breaks into hysterical laughter.

10. The Director covers his ears in humiliation and runs from the room.

Suggested Essay Topics

1. Compare the first four paragraphs in this chapter to the structure and society of a beehive. You will need to include a short explanation of a real beehive to make your comparison.

2. After Linda's entrance, the Director can only sputter a few phrases. Create an interior monologue of what could be going through his mind.

Chapter XI

New Characters:

Dr. Shaw: *the physician assigned to Linda*

Human Element Manager: *shows John the Electrical Equipment Corporation*

Dr. Gaffney: *Provost of Eton who shows John the school*

Miss Keate: *Head Mistress of Eton who attracts Bernard's attention*

Summary

Everyone in London knows about the Director's humiliation and wants to meet John. Linda is ignored in a hospital on a 24-hour *soma* holiday. Dr. Shaw admits to John that this will probably cause her death in a month. Since any rejuvenation is impossible, John accepts this.

Bernard's ego is fed by all those courting his favor to gain access to John. Women invite themselves into his bed and his early moral heresy is pushed aside. What is left is his hypocrisy. The whispers about mistakes in his blood surrogate return, and his reports to Mustapha Mond become more officious. This marks the beginning of Bernard's downfall, but it will happen according to Mond's schedule.

The two field trips that John makes continue Huxley's satire on a utopian world. John becomes physically nauseated at the lighting factory. He cannot understand the laughter of the children at Eton when slides of his own religious rites are shown, and he learns that reading is discouraged because it is done alone. Throughout the Eton visit, Bernard spends his time propositioning Miss Keate. Because he is successful with her, he must rid himself of the Savage. He stops on their way home to call Lenina, asking her to take the Savage to the feelies. During the stop, the Savage witnesses the daily *soma* rations being distributed.

Lenina feels privileged to take the Savage out in public and is congratulated by Fanny. She confesses she has not been able to go to bed with him and hopes this might encourage him. The theater is filled with pleasant synthetic aromas and music. The feely is satirically titled *Three Weeks in a Helicopter* and details the sexual adventures of a negro who kidnaps a Beta blonde and keeps her in a helicopter as his sexual toy. Every viewer is a part of the whole fantasy experience through the feely technology. While Lenina basks in a sexual afterglow, the Savage is humiliated. He remains in the copter cab, says goodnight, and leaves her at her apartment house. Back in his own room, he reads passages from *Othello* instead of *Romeo and Juliet.* John's disillusionment, which began with his tours in the morning, continues into the evening. He turns from Shakespeare's play about innocent young love to the darker play of lies, betrayal, and sexual suspicion.

Analysis

Everyone in London fawns all over John because he is something new and different. He has lost his name and is now identified as the Savage, just as people are identified by their castes. Identity in this world is assigned to a person; it is not what he/she creates independently. His mother Linda is still an outcast in what was once her own society because she is old and ugly—distasteful and disgusting in this seemingly perfect society. Her son is still young, strong, and beautiful and therefore, desirable. Encased in her 24-hour *soma* haze, Linda doesn't care about anything else. Dr. Shaw considers her an experiment in something he has never seen: senility. She is a lab rat in her cage.

Bernard is on a supreme egotistical high. All the attention he has ever wanted is being lavished on him; men want his friendship and women, his bed. At this point, Helmholtz Watson is the one in Bernard's life who sees the true sham of Bernard's position and who knows that people still talk about him behind his back. The other person who knows Bernard's tenuous hold on fame is Mustapha Mond. He reads Bernard's reports with a mixture of anger at the hypocritical pronouncements on society and with a perverse sense of happiness, knowing that he will soon bring Bernard down.

The assembly-line scene in the Electrical Equipment Corporation, with specifically conditioned and adapted Bokanovsky

Groups, is the first crack in the Savage's fantasy-dream world. "O brave new world...." now sticks in his throat and he must vomit it out.

In the Eton geography room, John witnesses his deep religious beliefs, born in the 25 years on the Reservation, becoming a thing of derision. None of this touches the man John has considered his savior because Bernard is too busy trying to bed Miss Keate. Today's Eton is an upper-class boys public (private in the United States) school where the best families send their children. It is a boarding school that basically raises and trains upper-class boys to take their proper place in English society. Aldous Huxley has kept his New World Eton for upper-caste education. The children returning from their Death Conditioning is a foreshadowing of what John will soon have to face with Linda.

Even though Lenina likes the Savage, she has no understanding of his standards of morality and his reasons for not going to bed with her. The feely echoes what today would be labelled as pornographic or X-rated. In 1932, the description of this scene would have been even more provocative, somewhat reminiscent of D. H. Lawrence and his notorious novel *Lady Chatterley's Lover* (1929), which was banned in various countries because of its sexually explicit scenes.

John's feelings and sexual attraction for Lenina are strong, but he cannot go against the morality he learned at the Reservation and his romantic sense of love from what he has read in Shakespeare. Back in his room, he chooses to read *Othello*, Shakespeare's play about the Moor who kills his wife out of jealousy and passion because he wrongly believes that she has been unfaithful. Is Lenina the sweet, virginal Juliet that John pictures or the whore of Othello's suspicions? John still sees her as the former.

Study Questions

1. Why does everyone want to meet John?

2. What is Linda's existence now? What will eventually happen to her?

3. How does Bernard make himself more self-important?

4. How does society label John?

5. What effect does the visit to the Electrical Equipment Corporation have on John?

6. What does Bernard do during the visit to Eton?

7. What are the only books in Eton's library? Why?

8. Why does Bernard want Lenina to take the Savage to the feelies?

9. What is the Savage's reaction to the feely?

10. Why is Lenina disappointed at the end of the chapter?

Answers

1. John is a real Savage, new and unusual like a new animal in a zoo.

2. Linda is in a constant *soma* holiday. Dr. Shaw says that such heavy intake will kill her in about a month or two.

3. Bernard sets himself up as guardian and agent for John. Everyone who wants to meet John has to go through Bernard.

4. John is now known as the Savage—a classification instead of a name.

5. The Savage cannot stand the robot-like twins mechanically doing their jobs. He runs outside and vomits.

6. Bernard spends the entire visit to Eton propositioning Miss Keate. He pays no attention to the Savage or to the effect of the visit on him.

7. The only books are scientific reference books. Reading is a solitary activity to be discouraged. Group activity like the feelies is encouraged.

8. Bernard has made an appointment with Miss Keate for that night and needs the Savage out of the way. He doesn't consider the effect the feelies might have on the Savage.

9. The Savage is embarrassed, disgusted, and ashamed not only at what he has seen, but because Lenina was with him.

10. Lenina thinks the Savage will now go to bed with her. Instead, he doesn't even leave the taxicopter, but goes to his room at Bernard's.

Suggested Essay Topics

1. In *The Merchant of Venice* (II, vii, 1-10) the three caskets, or small jewel boxes, are described. The man who wins Portia in marriage must choose the correct one. Each is engraved with a message and is of a different metal:

   Gold - "Who chooseth me shall gain what many men desire."

   Silver - "Who chooseth me shall get as much as he deserves."

   Lead - "Who chooseth me must give and hazard all he hath."

   The gold and silver ones contain messages which berate the chooser as one who judges by surface value only. The lead one contains Portia's portrait and a verse commending the chooser for seeing below the surface. How does this compare to the Savage's use of the word "caskets" for the containers of *soma* being handed out to the workers? How are these the gold and silver caskets, not the lead?

2. Put yourself in the Savage's place at the feelies and imagine how he must have felt about the whole experience adding to his conflict of emotions over Lenina.

3. Bernard's importance is from his association with the Savage, not for what he actually is. Describe someone you know who is important because of who he/she knows, not what he/she is. What is your opinion of this person?

Chapter XII

New Character:

Arch-Community-Songster of Canterbury: *the most important guest at Bernard's reception for the Savage*

Summary

It is the night of Bernard's most important reception to show off the Savage, but John will not come out of his room. Bernard shouts at him, even calls him John, but to no avail. He finally has to announce to the guests that the Savage will not appear. Everyone leaves, indignant and feeling they have been tricked. All the old rumors about Bernard become more vocal. The Arch-Community-Songster chastises Bernard for tricking everyone and then leaves with Lenina. Soon the room is empty. In despair, Bernard takes a large dose of *soma*. The Savage reads *Romeo and Juliet* alone in his room.

Mustapha Mond has just finished reading "A New Theory of Biology." He decides it must not be published and that the author needs to be transferred to St. Helena for the safety of society. With the Arch-Community-Songster, Lenina decides she needs *soma* to continue the evening. Bernard sleeps the night away in *soma* bliss.

The next morning, the Savage is sympathetic to Bernard, but says he liked Bernard better when Bernard was unhappy instead of happy with the sham he is now living. Bernard strikes back by blaming the Savage as the cause of all of the problems of last night, even though he knows the truth in the Savage's statement. Instead of accepting the truth, he wants revenge. Bernard tries to rebuild his neglected friendship with Helmholtz Watson. The offer is accepted by Helmholtz with no reproach, which also makes Bernard envious of one who can be so generous. At first, Bernard is completely oblivious to the fact that Helmholtz is also in trouble. He has written some rhymes he used in a lecture, "On the Use of Rhymes in Moral Propaganda and Advertisement." His rhymes were on being alone, and were against the conditioning sleep-teaching; he wrote them to see what the reaction of his class would be.

When Helmholtz and the Savage meet and like each other immediately, Bernard again feels jealous and left out. The closer those he considers his friends become, the more he resents it and depends on *soma* for escape. When the two compare their respective poetries, he tries to turn it into a joke. After several incidents like this, Helmholtz threatens to kick Bernard out if he interrupts again. One problem arises when the Savage is reading from *Romeo and Juliet*. During the scene where Juliet begs her mother not to force her to marry Paris, Helmholtz bursts into loud laughter over the use of mother and father and the idea of a girl being forced to have someone she doesn't want. The Savage does not understand the ridicule. Helmholtz tries to explain that one has to be hurt and upset to think, but a situation like Juliet's will not work in this New World.

Analysis

The euphoria that Bernard has been experiencing comes crashing down around him just as the Savage's disillusionment with a society he had envisioned as perfect crashes in on him. All the important people at Bernard's reception come only to meet the Savage. Lenina takes his refusal to appear as a personal comment on her and feels physically ill. Since she has never in her life felt any deep human emotion, except those which were chemically induced, she doesn't recognize the effect of her nascent feelings. Lenina uses the name John, not Savage, but unlike Bernard, she means the use of the personal name. This New World has not been successful in ridding its people of their emotions, only in covering them over with chemical surrogates to flush these socially-upsetting emotions from the body immediately. The shallow, sycophantic attitude of Bernard's guests is evident as they whisper and gossip overtly about mistakes on Bernard's embryo. The most important guest, the Arch-Community-Songster of Canterbury, solemnly berates Bernard for his actions. In England, the Archbishop of Canterbury is the head of the Church of England and is a most influential person. The Songster is a parody of this office. He pontificates at Bernard as if he were an unruly child or an unrepentant sinner, then majestically sweeps from the room with Lenina.

The character of Mond is more fully developed as the reader begins to see a person who is a Controller in all senses of the word; he is a censor who can decide the fate of any dissident at any time. Mustapha Mond's censoring of the paper he has been reading foreshadows the fall of another important person, but who? The reader is left to guess. Helmholtz's statement from an earlier chapter has proven true; words are like x-rays, and Mond wants to make sure that none of those x-ray words pierce the smooth surface of the New World. The stability must not be upset.

The Savage has tried to forget the Lenina that led him to *Othello* and has returned to *Romeo and Juliet*, perhaps imagining John and Lenina. This is his attempt at self-conditioning, just as he had to create his own religion and initiation in Malpais.

Bernard's deflated ego loses itself in the *soma* dreams against which he had once railed. He is not the romantic, Byronic hero he has tried to imagine himself as. As soon as he thought he was accepted into society, he accepted all of that society's amenities. Rather than seeing the reality of his position, Bernard reverts to his usual method of assigning blame to everyone else, mainly to the Savage. He is like a child who says, "Not me!" and points to someone else. He had once condemned the child-like instant gratification of his world, but he cannot advance beyond it himself. For all his criticism of his society, Bernard is the most superficial of all the characters in the novel.

Bernard's attempt at renewal of his friendship with Helmholtz is doomed also. Helmholtz and the Savage are men who have found their solace in words. It is words that have been their true friend in their lives as social outcasts, and it is words that have caused most of their problems. To create and enjoy words, one must think, and thinking often takes one outside the accepted norm of society. It is only natural that words bridge the gap between the two worlds of these men, and that Bernard remain on the outside. In fact, Bernard is secretly happy at the problems Helmholtz's words have caused him. When Bernard is miserable, he rejoices at another's unhappy situation. Helmholtz is still a product of his society and cannot go beyond Juliet's words to her mother to see the anguish of her situation. But he does understand that there needs to be a hurtful and upsetting situation to get people to realize the power in words; he just doesn't know what situation would work in his world.

Study Questions

1. What important person has Bernard invited to his reception? Why?

2. How do the people at the reception feel when the Savage doesn't appear?

3. How does Lenina feel?

4. What is the Savage reading? Why?

5. How does Bernard cope with the failure of the evening?

6. To whom does Bernard try to turn?

7. What is Helmholtz's situation? Why?

8. What happens when Bernard tries to interrupt Helmholtz and the Savage?

9. What makes Helmholtz laugh at *Romeo and Juliet*?

10. What does Helmholtz say his society needs?

Answers

1. Bernard has tried to make an impression by inviting the Arch-Community-Songster of Canterbury to his reception.

2. Bernard's guests feel cheated and tricked. They came to meet the Savage, not to have to put up with Bernard.

3. Lenina feels hurt, empty, and physically ill. She thinks the Savage doesn't want to see her personally.

4. The Savage reads *Romeo and Juliet*. He wants to see himself as Romeo and Lenina as Juliet.

5. Bernard blames the Savage for the evening's failure and takes *soma*.

6. Bernard tries to renew his friendship with Helmholtz Watson now that he is an outcast again.

7. Some of Helmholtz's rhymes have been about being alone, and he is in trouble with the authorities.

8. Helmholtz threatens to remove Bernard from the room if he interrupts again.

9. Juliet's reference to her mother and her situation of being forced to accept a man against her will is too foreign to Helmholtz for him to take seriously.

10. Helmholtz says his society needs some kind of madness and violence to shake it up.

Suggested Essay Topics

1. How does the Savage compare his situation to Romeo and romantically view Lenina as Juliet?

2. There have been many historical instances of leaders burning books in an attempt to keep socially rebellious ideas from spreading into society. One is Hitler's burning of books. A modern novel based on this idea is *Fahrenheit 451*. Why and how are words dangerous?

3. How has Bernard become a double outcast by his society? By Helmholtz and the Savage?

Chapter XIII

Summary

Henry Foster invites Lenina to a feely and she turns him down. She does not look well, and Henry begins suggesting all the standard chemical solutions. She becomes angry and forgets to give an embryo the proper sleeping sickness injection. Later, in the Changing Room, Fanny is incredulous that Lenina has let herself get into such a state over one man with whom she hasn't even gone to bed. *Soma* doesn't even work anymore. Fanny advises Lenina to seduce the Savage.

Lenina dresses herself carefully and pays a surprise visit to John. He is so overwhelmed he falls to his knees in front of her and says he feels unworthy. He tries to explain the customs from Malpais in which a man proved himself to the woman he wanted. Lenina has no clue as to the meaning of his words. He talks of marriage and monogamy, which she calls horrible. She only senses his sexual need for her and none of his romantic fantasy or morality. She begins to undress and stands naked in front of him. As she moves toward him, he backs away like a terrified animal. The harder she tries with her seduction, the more panic-stricken he becomes. Suddenly, the word "whore" comes from his mouth. First he shakes her, then slaps her and orders her to go. Lenina rushes for the safety of the locked bathroom.

John paces outside the door, vehemently reciting Shakespeare's lines on the vileness of woman. Lenina finally convinces him to push her clothes through the ventilator. She is now dressed, but terrified to come out. She hears John answer the phone and speak very excitedly. After she hears the front door slam, she cautiously comes from the bathroom, listens, runs through the deserted living room and into the lift. Only then does she feel safe.

Analysis

This chapter is the climax of the relationship between John and Lenina, and ultimate clash of their cultures and ingrained beliefs about life. John has been just as conditioned by his society and his Shakespeare as Lenina has by genetic engineering and

hypnopaedia. The two can never understand each other. In reality, no woman can live up to John's highly romanticized ideal, nor live on the pedestal of his fantasy. He has become Pygmalion, but his ideal has not brought him satisfaction. Pygmalion was the Greek sculptor who made a statue of the perfect woman. A goddess breathed life into her and she became the sculptor's perfect wife. John's perfect woman in Lenina is an illusion. Lenina's overt seduction sickens him and his own sexual urges betray his morality. He cannot accept this or Lenina's "feet of clay." One more crack has opened up in this New World, and all is falling in on itself like a collapsing star. Romeo and his Juliet are gone, to be replaced once more by the jealous raving of Othello. Instead of a sexual climax bringing them together as Lenina had hoped, an emotional climax has ripped them apart.

Study Questions

1. What does Henry Foster recommend for Lenina's condition?
2. Because she is upset, what does Lenina forget?
3. What does Fanny advise Lenina?
4. Whom had John been expecting when Lenina visits him?
5. What does John do when he sees Lenina?
6. What does John want to do for Lenina?
7. What does Lenina try to do to seduce John?
8. What idea does Lenina find horrible?
9. What does John finally do to Lenina?
10. What distracts John from his murderous rage?

Answers

1. Henry recommends that Lenina have a Pregnancy Substitute or a Violent Passion Surrogate.
2. Lenina is so angry that she forgets to give an embryo an immunization against sleeping sickness.

3. Fanny advises Lenina to make a move and seduce the Savage.

4. The Savage thought Helmholtz was at the door.

5. John drops to his knees in front of Lenina.

6. John wants to perform some physical task to prove he is worthy of her.

7. Lenina embraces and tries to kiss John, then strips naked in front of him.

8. John wants Lenina to marry him and to live with him forever.

9. John shakes Lenina, then slaps her and tells her to leave.

10. A telephone call that seems to be about something important causes John to leave the apartment.

Suggested Essay Topics

1. In Greek mythology, the sculptor Pygmalion creates a statue of the perfect woman, then falls in love with her. He prays to Venus to send him love. When he returns from the temple, his beautiful statue has become his beautiful and loving wife. Compare and contrast this myth and its outcome to the woman John wants Lenina to be and its probable outcome.

2. Is Lenina wrong in her approach to John in light of the society in which she has grown up? How has this led to her misunderstanding of him?

Chapter XIV

New Character:

Nurse: *attending nurse in Ward 81; she does not understand John's concern about Linda.*

Summary

John has arrived at the Park Lane Hospital for the Dying. Linda is in Ward 81 with 19 others and all the scent, sight, and sound conveniences. The nurse cannot understand the Savage's concern and anxiety. When he says Linda is his mother, the nurse blushes in embarrassment, but takes him to her. For everyone else there, galloping senility does not allow time for any signs of aging, unlike Linda. The nurse briskly walks away down the row of beds. Linda is propped up in a bed at the end of the ward next to the wall. She dozes in and out of a *soma* haze to gaze vaguely at the small television on the foot of her bed while music plays softly and aromas drift through the air. She has an infantile look on her old face. Because she has other duties, the nurse leaves the Savage alone with Linda.

Sitting beside the bed, the Savage takes Linda's hand and calls her name. She seems to recognize him but then drifts back to sleep again. He remembers the good times with her from his childhood and tears come to his eyes. The quiet is suddenly shattered by the shrill voices of children. A group of khaki-clad Delta children, identical boys, crowd around all the beds laughing and playing. When they reach Linda's bed, they are rudely curious, commenting on her physical appearance. One squeezes up between the Savage's chair and Linda's bed to stare at Linda's face. This is too much. The Savage lifts him over the chair, boxes his ears, and makes the child cry. The nurse comes running and scolds him. She tells him the children are being death-conditioned and he is the one who will have to go. He steps toward her and she sends the twins away.

The Savage tries to recapture the moment he had with Linda, but now memories of Popé and a neglectful mother, dirt, flies, and hurtful names fill his mind. When Linda does not recognize her son, he shakes her, shouting his name. She begins gasping for breath, her lips turn blue, and a terrified look is in her eyes. The ward nurse is surrounded by a group of Delta twins undergoing death conditioning, and is not happy with the Savage's emotional behavior. The twins watch with interest as the Savage falls to his knees and cries at Linda's deathbed. As the nurse tries to distract the Deltas with chocolate, John becomes more emotional. When two of the twins ask if Linda is dead with a very matter-of-fact tone, the Savage roughly pushes one of them to the floor and walks to the door at the end of the ward.

Analysis

The phone call from the previous chapter is to inform the Savage that Linda is dying. His reaction is what today's reader would consider normal: concern, sadness, pain. However, to the world he has chosen to enter, the world of his dreams, he is an oddity to be scorned. Ward 81 is a synthetic attempt at pleasantness. Nurses are professional and efficient. There really is not much to do. Galloping senility does away with any problems associated with dying in a quick, efficient manner, the same way life is lived; no mess, no fuss. The Savage's concern surprises the nurse, but his statement, "She's my mother," totally horrifies her.

Even in her dying, Linda is on the fringe of society in a bed at the far end of the ward, just as her hut at Malpais was removed from the pueblo. She is the least visible and therefore the least upsetting to see, even though there are few visitors. Since there is no emotional closeness during life, there is little sense of loss in death. Childhood death conditioning ensures this. Linda's oblivious sleep-dreamstate further alienates the Savage from his one last link with his past. She is perhaps the only person who has ever loved him, and she doesn't even recognize him. The *soma* that has given her a kind of personal bliss has shut him out. It is her Indian lover Popé who fills her mind, not her son.

At first, the only memories the Savage has of his mother are loving ones. He recalls the strange mixture of songs and stories, the way she painted the Other Place as perfect. He has seen the ugly imperfections and this suddenly crashes in on his private moment as the horde of Delta twins crowd around. Once again, the two societies clash. The children are only following their own conditioning as the Savage is following his. Our sympathy probably lies with him, and the children seem rude and intrusive.

In one way, they are being normal children, curious and unaware of the situation and the emotion involved. Nowhere is any kind of afterlife mentioned: a person lives and a person dies. Enjoyment and pleasure during life is everything. Dead bodies are recyclable elements to be cremated and, in death, still benefit all of society.

The intrusion of the children on the Savage's reverie erases the pleasant memories. Popé's cruelty and his mother's neglect and drunkenness are all he can remember. The final insult and rejection is when Linda calls her own son Popé. Her son has become the intruder, again the unwanted one. All his mother wants is the pleasure of the moment. Now it is anger that fills him as he grabs and shakes his mother. This action will add to his feelings of guilt. He still carries guilt over his attraction to Lenina; now he will carry the misplaced guilt that he caused Linda's death. In reality, his action probably hastened her death by a few moments, but the fact that he was called by the hospital confirms that she was already dying. His mental and emotional burdens are piling up on him. To add to this, his emotional actions are being criticized and scrutinized instead of comforted.

Bernard's professed friendship is a sham. Lenina has become a wanton whore. Helmholtz has laughed at the human situations in Shakespeare's plays. Linda dies with the name of her Indian lover on her lips. John has no one and no place.

Study Questions

1. What is Ward 81 like?

2. What shocks and embarrasses the nurse?

3. In what condition is Linda?

4. What are John's first memories as he sits at Linda's bedside?

5. What disturbs the Savage's memories?

6. How does the Savage react when one boy squeezes up beside him?

7. How does the nurse try to pacify the children?

8. Whose name does Linda speak? What does this do to John?

9. What upsets the nurse when the Savage shouts for her to come to Linda?

10. How does the Savage leave the ward?

Answers

1. Ward 81 is synthetically pleasing with music, aromas, and television. Everything is in bright colors.

2. The Savage says that Linda is his mother.

3. Linda is in her *soma* dreams, unaware of everything around her.

4. John remembers the Linda who sang to him and told him stories and, in her own way, loved him.

5. The group of Delta twins crowd into the ward for their death conditioning.

6. The Savage grabs the boy, slaps him, and makes him cry.

7. The nurse offers chocolate to try to distract the children.

8. Linda speaks the name Popé. This upsets John and makes him angry.

9. The nurse doesn't want the children upset and perhaps deconditioned.

10. The Savage shoves the children, knocking one down, and storms out of the ward.

Suggested Essay Topics

1. Keeping Linda in her *soma* dreams even though it will bring about her death more quickly raises ethical questions about patient treatment. Is it ethical to do what makes a dying patient comfortable, even if it hastens that person's death?

2. Compare and contrast the Savage's attitude about Linda's dying with that of the nurse and the children. Keep in mind this is not a question of right or wrong, but of a difference of cultures.

3. Discuss how Linda's lack of recognition of her own son leads to his further feeling of rejection.

Chapter XV

New Character:

The Deputy Sub-Bursar: *he is called to distribute* soma *to the workers; he also calls Bernard about the Savage.*

Summary

The Savage steps out of the lift (elevator) into a group of Bokanovsky Group menial workers who are finishing their shift. They are receiving their daily *soma* rations. He pushes through them, not realizing where he is. The mirror-image workers begin to squeak at him and elbow him for disturbing them. He is reminded of maggots as he looks at them. He keeps repeating his mantra-like quote from *The Tempest*, but there is no comfort. The *soma* box is carried in and the Savage is forgotten as the twins obediently fall into line. The Savage keeps repeating his phrase, but it still doesn't work. The Deputy Sub-Bursar threatens to stop the *soma* distribution and the Delta twins quiet down.

Unable to contain himself any longer, the Savage rushes to the table calling, "Stop!" He begs the twins to stop poisoning themselves. The Sub-Bursar politely tries to move him away and quiet him. The Savage starts telling the twins to throw the *soma* away. This simple command penetrates their minds and they become restless and confused. A real problem is developing and the Sub-Bursar goes to the telephone to look up Bernard's number.

Bernard cannot find the Savage at home. He and Helmholtz have been looking for him so they can all go to dinner. When Bernard answers the telephone, he becomes very agitated and angry. He and Helmholtz leave for the Park Lane Hospital.

The Savage is preaching freedom and rebellion to a petrified group of Delta twins. He begins to throw the *soma* baskets out the window. This upsets everyone. Bernard walks in and fears for the Savage's life. He and Helmholtz push through the crowd. The *soma* is gone and the Delta twins are furious. Helmholtz makes his way to the Savage, but Bernard hesitates on the edge of the crowd, not wanting to risk getting involved. Instead he runs around shouting, "Help!" pretending he is doing something.

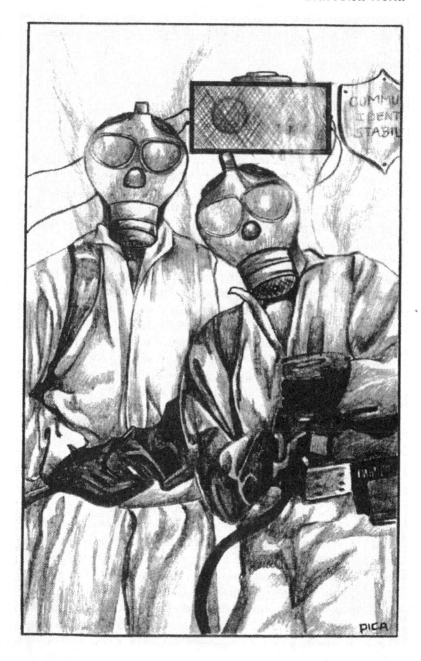

Gas-masked policemen rush in with spraying machines, pumping *soma* into the air. They also carry water pistols filled with anesthetic. People begin to crumple to the floor. Then the Voice of Reason begins to come from the Synthetic Music Box, speaking of peace and happiness. Soon, all are in tears and hugging each other. Finally, all the Deltas are sedated and gone. The Sergeant begins to lead the Savage and Helmholtz away. Bernard tries to move unobserved toward the door. The Sergeant puts his hand on Bernard's shoulder to prevent his escape, which Bernard denies. He finally admits he is a friend of the Savage and joins the other two.

Utopia must be forcefully maintained, sometimes violently and physically. Any hint of discord is quashed with drugs and psycho-suggestion. The end justifies the means to preserve stability.

Analysis

Having been pushed to his emotional limit, the Savage's intrusion on the mirror-image Deltas and their *soma* distribution is the snapping point. "O brave new world..." has turned to ashes in his mouth. Linda had been a slave to *soma* and it killed her. In his mind, all have become slaves and it is his duty to free them. His passion and naiveté have made him forget that the Delta twins do not have the basic intelligence to understand what he is talking about. They are only disturbed by the upheaval in their orderly world.

Knowing Bernard's past, it is difficult to tell if he is more concerned about the Savage or his own reputation. By the end of the chapter, it is clear that he is out for himself. He stays on the outside of the group swirling around the Savage and Helmholtz. He runs toward the gas-masked police looking self-important, but trying not to look as if he is a part of the melee. His attempt to escape shows him for the coward that he is. He resigns himself to arrest.

If this New World is so perfect, why are riot police fitted with gas masks, *soma* spray, and anesthetic so quickly available? The riot police are ever alert to quash the least bit of rebellion and to drug away any threat to stability. Once in a drugged and receptive mood, the hypnopaedic Voice of Reason latches into previous conditioning and all is subdued until the next time. Nothing of these episodes is ever made public, and others blissfully continue with their lives. All seems to end quietly, but it is the lull before the storm. This incident cannot be glossed over by those at the top, especially Mustapha Mond.

Study Questions

1. Why isn't the Savage aware of the crowd around him?

2. How do the Delta twins react to the Savage's pushing through?

3. To what does the Savage compare the Delta twins?

4. What does the Deputy Sub-Bursar threaten if the group doesn't settle down?

5. What does the Savage do with the *soma* boxes?

6. Whom does the Sub-Bursar call? Why?

7. What does Helmholtz do at the hospital?

8. Why are the Delta twins truly upset?

9. How do the police subdue the crowd?

10. What does the Sergeant do?

Answers

1. The Savage is grief-stricken and remorseful over Linda's death.

2. The Deltas are upset because their routine is upset.

3. The Savage says the Deltas are like maggots swarming over Linda's body.

4. The Sub-Bursar closes the cash box and threatens to stop the *soma* distribution.

5. The Savage throws the *soma* boxes out the window.

6. The Sub-Bursar calls Bernard because he thinks he is the Savage's friend.

7. Helmholtz pushes through the crowd to join the Savage.

8. The Deltas are the most upset with the *soma* ration being gone.

9. The riot police use *soma* spray and anesthetic-loaded water pistols on the crowd.

10. The Sergeant takes the Savage, Helmholtz, and Bernard into custody.

Suggested Essay Topics

1. Discuss why the words of the Savage have no effect on the Delta twins. What is the only thing that moves them to action, and why is his, "Throw it away!" such a powerful statement for them? Remember the conditioning scene in chapter II.

2. "'O brave new world!' It was a challenge, a command." What is the Savage's challenge?

3. In Chapter X, the Director had called the Hatchery a "hive of industry." In this chapter, the Savage calls the Deltas a group of maggots climbing over Linda's body. Compare and contrast the two statements.

Chapter XVI

Summary

Bernard, Helmholtz, and the Savage are ushered into Mustapha Mond's office. Bernard takes the most uncomfortable chair as far back in the room as possible. Helmholtz seats himself in the most comfortable chair, and the Savage paces the room. He pages through a Bible-like book for the New World, *My Life and Work* by Our Ford, but finds it uninteresting.

As he enters, Mond's first sentence is to the Savage, stating truthfully the Savage's dislike for this society. Quoting Shakespeare, Mond says that he is one of the few who has read the plays. He reminds Bernard that since he makes the rules, he can also break them. When Helmholtz admits he would like to write something like *Othello*, Mond tells him he never will because there is no understanding of the emotions involved. High art is old and beautiful and must be sacrificed for stability. People of assigned intelligences cannot be discontented with assigned tasks.

Mond then relates the details of the Cyprus experiment to prove his point. A group of Alphas was placed on an island with everything necessary to create a civilization. In six years, violent civil war had broken out and those who were left petitioned the World Controllers to take charge. He compares society to an iceberg with eight-ninths of the people below the waterline: childish, happy, provided for. Science must also be censored, and Mond admits that at one point he went too far and risked exile. Bernard is sentenced to Iceland. Mond relates a brief history of the problems of the past 600 years since Our Ford, with the turning point at the Nine Years' War. This caused a desire for stability and an acceptance of total control that has remained. Helmholtz chooses an inhospitable climate for his place of exile, and is sent to the Falkland Islands.

Analysis

When the Savage and Helmholtz muse about rewriting Shakespeare's plays, Mond's answer is, "...you can't make tragedies without social instability." The words on the shield over the Hatchery are Community, Identity, Stability. In this chapter, much of the phi-

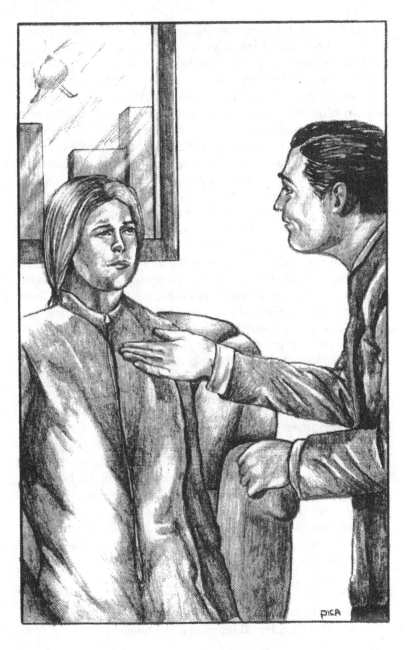

losophy behind this New World is revealed with Mustapha Mond as its narrator. If all is kept only surface-deep and people are kept thinking they are happy with *soma* and circuses, then they will not realize the shallowness of their own lives. Mond admits, "Happiness is never grand." One way of ensuring happiness is to keep the majority of the population, the eight-ninths, at a mental level where they are always happy with what their places are in society and do not desire more. The more sheep-like a person is, the easier he/she is to control. If this is enhanced with psychological conditioning, the perfect society is created. Mond's description of the Cyprus experiment demonstrates this. It is generally less taxing to be told what to do, especially if one is allowed the seeming freedom to find pleasure whenever and with whomever one wants. A human being's emotions and desires can become the inspiration of the greatest hopes or deepest miseries. First, any religion that curbs those desires must be done away with, allowing people free rein. Condition them to rid themselves of any uneasiness resulting from indulgence with chemical bliss. Carefully control anything that might upset the equation: high art, science, even work. Give each human a sense of purpose, or artificial identity, and make him/her feel that identity is a part of a community.

In any society, there are leaders and followers. While leaders enjoy privileges that followers don't, they also sacrifice something of themselves for their positions. Mond gave up his science for leadership. "Happiness is a hard master, particularly other people's happiness." However, Mond's self-sacrifice almost seems like a self-crucifixion, perhaps similar to what John tried to achieve on the Reservation. Mond relishes his position and the fact that he knows secrets that no one else does. In some ways, he is not as noble as he appears. He delights in the power he has to determine how society will live, to say words like mother or father, to experience beauty, to send Bernard and Helmholtz into exile, to continue his experiment with the Savage.

Study Questions

1. When Bernard, Helmholtz, and the Savage are ushered into Mond's office, how does each place himself?

2. How does Mond greet the Savage?

3. Why are things like Shakespeare's plays prohibited?

4. Why can't *Othello* be rewritten?

5. Why can't a world of Alphas be created?

6. What proved that an Alpha society would fail?

7. Why are some labor-saving devices not put to use?

8. What is Bernard's reaction to exile?

9. What event changed people's ideas about truth and beauty?

10. For what does Helmholtz ask? Where is he to be sent?

Answers

1. Bernard tries to be as inconspicuous as possible. Helmholtz confidently sits in the best chair. The Savage paces restlessly.

2. Mond walks directly to the Savage and speaks of his discontent with society.

3. Shakespeare's plays are beautiful, old, and wasteful.

4. Tragedies like *Othello* require social instability. Stability is one of the watchwords of this society.

5. Alphas would be unhappy doing menial jobs and that would breed discontent.

6. The Cyprus experiment proved an Alpha society would fail.

7. People must have a certain percentage of their days taken up with what must seem to be meaningful work. Labor-saving devices could take this away.

8. Bernard begs not to be taken away and is carried out crying.

9. The Nine Years' War caused people to desire control to keep such slaughter from happening again.

10. Helmholtz wants to go to a place where the climate is bad because he thinks it will be a more creative atmosphere. He will be sent to the Falkland Islands.

Suggested Essay Topics

1. Mond states, "...and you can't make tragedies without social instability." What does he mean? Do you agree or disagree? Explain.

2. The Cyprus experiment failed and ended in civil war. Early experiments in social communism failed because the groups were all intellectuals and no one wanted to work. Use the problems Mond described in the Cyprus experiment and show how these are typical problems in an intellectual, and therefore unstable, society.

3. Society at the end of the twentieth century seems to be more unstable and unproductive than earlier in the century. Could this lead to a Brave New World society?

4. "Beauty is truth, truth beauty—that is all ye know on earth, and all ye need to know."—John Keats "Ode on a Grecian Urn"

   "Universal happiness keeps the wheels steadily turning; truth and beauty can't."— Mustapha Mond

   John Keats' quote is a romantic view of the world; Mond's is a realistic one. Compare and contrast the two. Is there a happy medium?

Chapter XVII

Summary

The Savage and Mond continue their discussion alone, with the topic turning to religion. Using a Bible and several books of religious commentaries, Mond comments that even though God doesn't change, man does. He points out that since this New Utopian World has youth and scientific prosperity, it doesn't need God. He isn't compatible with machinery, science, and happiness. The Savage then raises the question of unending happiness as a way of degrading man. Mond answers that degradation depends on the standards society sets, and that self-indulgence is needed for successful industrial consumerism. Conditioning makes everyone do what ought to be done with no room for heroism or nobility. *Soma* removes any moments of doubt and Violent Passion Surrogate replaces the vague human urge for the adrenaline rush connected with danger.

Undefeated, the Savage claims the right to be unhappy and inconvenienced. Mond grants his wish.

Analysis

John Henry, Cardinal Newman (1801-1890), was an Anglican clergyman who later converted to Catholicism. He believed that man was not made for independence, but belongs to God.

Newman speaks of man belonging to God. However, the idea has been adulterated to mean, "Everyone belongs to everyone else." Mond says that God does not change, but civilization does. God has been replaced by the good of society. Karl Marx wrote, "Religion...is the opiate of the people." *Soma* has replaced religion and opium. As was seen in the previous chapters, the book *My Life and Work* by Our Ford has been designed to look like the Bible. The sign of the T has replaced the sign of the cross. The rites of the Solidarity Group have replaced the rite of communion. Religion has not truly disappeared; it has been changed, bastardized. The need for sacred rites has not changed, but the object of veneration has.

Another writing Mond uses, by Maine de Biran, states that man ages and passions cool, "God emerges as from behind a cloud...."

The answer to this is to keep people young, involved, immersed in sensual pleasures, and never alone; then there is no time to contemplate the eternal. Science and machinery have become the god of this society. No one is allowed to suffer or be unhappy; so there is no need to call on the support of a higher power. It is the standards of society that determine when a man will feel degraded and when he will feel happy: a type of situation ethics. With no obstacles to overcome, no self-denial to torture man, there is no need for nobility and heroism. The dragons have all been slain—or exiled. Horrible as it is, what is humanity ready to give up to never have war? Chemical calming, *soma*, chemical purging, and Violent Passion Surrogate give man instant respite from all his pain and suffering, but at what price? Who determines what direction society will take? To achieve peace and contentment, should man put his life in the hands of a few? The Savage chooses not to lose control of his life, the right to be unhappy, to shed tears, to reach out and touch life—even if some of it is ugly. He has rejected the creatures he found in the Brave New World.

This dialogue between Mond and the Savage reveals the replacement of religion and God by science. The Chapter XVI discussion was on happiness and social stability. Huxley, during his life, isolated himself from society and withdrew into a type of Hindu contemplation. Since Mond will not grant exile to the Savage, like Huxley, the Savage chooses to exile himself.

Study Questions

1. In the New World, where is God and where is Ford?

2. To whom does Mond compare Cardinal Newman?

3. Whose property does Newman say man is?

4. When does de Biran say man finds God?

5. When does Mond say man can be independent from God?

6. What attitude of society does Mond say keeps the wheels turning?

7. What has society done with what the Savage calls the "slings and arrows of outrageous fortune"?

8. When the Savage thinks of unpleasant things, what does he remember?

9. What replaces living dangerously?

10. What does the Savage choose?

Answers

1. God is in the safe. Ford is on the shelves.

2. Mond compares Cardinal Newman to the Arch-Community-Songster.

3. Newman says that man is God's property.

4. De Biran says that as man ages and youthful passions cool, he finds God.

5. Mond says that when man has youth and prosperity for his whole life he can do without God.

6. Self-indulgence keeps the wheels turning, not self-denial.

7. Society has removed all the bad things and everything which is unpleasant. Life is too easy.

8. The Savage remembers Linda's dying, and the mocking laughter at her appearance.

9. Violent Passion Surrogate gives an instant adrenaline rush to replace any desire for danger.

10. The Savage chooses the right to be unhappy.

Suggested Essay Topics

1. At Malpais, the Savage suffered as an outcast from the pueblo. In the civilized world, he suffers from never being alone. Show how the need to be with others and the need to be alone are part of being human, but must be kept in balance.

2. Mond says that in this world there are no losses to compensate for; youthful desires never fail, minds and bodies continue to delight in activity, and *soma* takes care of any problems. While this may sound like paradise, is it truly the best

way to live? Can a man really know that he is happy if he has never been unhappy? Include the Savage's statement, "Nothing costs enough here."

3. "But I don't want comfort. I want God, I want Poetry, I want real danger, I want freedom, I want goodness. I want sin." Why does the Savage choose this even though he witnessed all this his first 25 years of life and thought he wanted to be done with it?

Chapter XVIII

New Characters:

Darwin Bonaparte: *secretly photographs the Savage like a wild animal photographer would*

Reporters from the various news services who try to interview the Savage

Summary

Helmholtz and Bernard find Bernard's apartment door open and the sound of vomiting coming from the bathroom. Helmholtz calls the Savage by name, John. John comes from the bathroom. He has purged himself with an emetic of mustard water. The two men have come to say good-bye because they begin their exile the next morning. The three are sad but somehow realize they are also happy. Even though he asked, John will not be allowed to join one of them in exile because Mond has said he wants to continue the experiment. John refuses to remain an experiment.

The Savage leaves London and travels to an abandoned lighthouse on the English coastline near Portsmouth. This will be his place of exile and is seemingly lonely and desolate. It is as far away as he can get without leaving England. His first night is spent praying, and putting himself through physical torment. The next morning he realizes that the lighthouse is still too much a part of what he has been trying to leave behind, but the site is beautiful. From the highest platform of the lighthouse he can still see some civilization, but on the ground all seems to disappear. He has brought some supplies with him, but he is determined to use as little synthetic and surrogate as possible. He plants a garden and makes a bow and arrows to shoot game. He finds himself singing and happy as he busies himself in productive work. Then he realizes that he has forgotten Linda and her suffering. He makes the mustard emetic again and beats himself with a whip of knotted cords. Unknown to him, he is observed by three Delta land workers.

Three days later, reporters appear as the Savage is making his arrows. One tries to question him for a radio broadcast. The Savage shouts Indian curse words and literally kicks the reporter's backside. Sensational headlines spread across London and are picked up by major reporters from all over the Western world. Four more reporters appear and try to question him. He chases them away with a thick switch. He pierces one helicopter with an arrow. After that, the helicopters keep out of bow-shot, but buzz like mosquitos in the distance.

Once, while he is working in his garden, the Savage has visions of Lenina as she tried to seduce him. In penance, he flings himself into a clump of spiked juniper bushes. This is not enough to purge his desire and he begins to whip himself as her memory lingers. He must humiliate himself in an attempt to atone for his lustful thoughts.

In a blind much like a hunter would use in stalking game, a photographer, Darwin Bonaparte, chronicles all the Savage's self-torment on film. He has also placed hidden microphones all around the Savage's home. Twelve days later, *The Savage of Surrey* has become a feely in all of Western Europe. This brings swarms of helicopters filled with people who want to see the Savage for themselves. He compares them to swarms of flies around a dead thing. His place of retreat has become a place of amusement, like a zoo. *Soma* and sex chewing gum are thrown down to him. They chant to see him whip himself. One helicopter lands and a young woman emerges. The Savage goes after her with a whip and she runs for the helicopter and the protection of her companion, but he runs behind the helicopter. The Savage turns the whip on himself. The crowds of people push forward and begin to mimic his gestures and torment as if it is a live feely. Like the climax of a Solidarity

Group meeting, someone begins to chant the rhythmic "orgy-porgy."

The Savage awakens the next day in the heather, still under the lingering effects of *soma* and hours of orgiastic frenzy. He is horrified and filled with self-loathing. That evening, when the helicopters return, filled with people ready for another night of revelry, no one answers their calls. Inside the lighthouse they find the Savage hanging from the highest rafters in the arch.

Analysis

The Savage has been repulsed by all he has learned from his discussion with Mustapha Mond. His emetic of mustard is an attempt to purge himself physically as well as mentally. This is a practice that will continue until his death. The last meeting of Helmholtz, Bernard, and the Savage is one of a sense of loss, something the first two have never truly known. Yet this sense of loss makes them feel more human and, in that, there is a sense of happiness; they do finally feel human emotions and understand that humans can be silent with each other because in that silence there is real sharing.

The Savage does not realize that his attempt at escape is just another part of Mond's experiment. The fact that Mond is willing to sacrifice the life of the Savage for the sake of scientific curiosity and propaganda shows that he is not as noble and self-sacrificing as he has portrayed himself. His discussions with the Savage have convinced him that John is the grit in the oyster shell of his world that could cause a pearl of great price that Mond does not want. He is not willing to sell his world and his position of control for such a gem. However, exile, which would remove the Savage from his control and execution, is out of the question. Mond must realize what the end will be because he knows John so well. All he has to do is sit back and wait. Then he can exploit the situation to show the world that his control is better, using John's suicide as propaganda.

The self-flagellation of the Savage echoes the actions of the groups of flagellates who wandered the medieval world, whipping themselves to atone for their own sins and the sins of the world. No matter which society he has been in, he has been denied any rites of passage. He has had to initiate his own rites and methods of sacrifice, a combination of the lore of the pueblo and Linda's mythology of the Other Place. His purging and whipping are methods of penance, but is there true penitence? Instead of unhappiness leading to happiness, his moments of happiness take him into torment.

One wonders if the appearance of the Delta-Minus land workers who discover the Savage is happenstance or has been engineered by Mond. In any event, the result is just what Mond had hoped for. The Savage has become a new entertainment and curiosity, like the blind dancing bear in a street circus. Even though he tries to create a situation of torment and penance from the situation, he only makes himself more of a spectacle. The name of the Feely Corporation's photographer, Darwin Bonaparte, blends the author of the theory of evolution with the man who wanted to be the emperor of all Europe in the name of Liberte, Egalite, Fraternitie. All through the novel, Aldous Huxley has used character names that echo historical dictators and political revolutionaries: Marx, Benito, Darwin, Bonaparte.

Though the young woman who steps from the helicopter is not identified as Lenina, from her actions and the reactions of the Savage, it is obvious. The man who deserts her to her fate is Henry Foster. The Savage hurls his Shakespearean epithets at her, then begins his whipping. Once again there is penance, but human desire overtakes penitence and ends in orgy. He has been unable to rid himself of one of the most basic human urges. The only penance left is self-destruction.

This is the denouenment, the unraveling of the plot, and perhaps the only possible outcome. Mond has an example to hold up to his utopian society without creating a martyr. John's suicide is not only the destruction of *an* individual, but of *the* individual to Huxley's view of utopia. In the first paragraph of the novel, the shield on the Hatchery states, "Community, Identity, Stability." Identity must come from the Community, not the individual, to preserve the Stability.

Study Questions

1. What is the Savage doing when Bernard and Helmholtz come to say goodbye?

2. When do the two men leave to begin their exile?

3. What does the Savage plan to do? Why?

4. Where does the Savage go for his self-exile?

5. How does the Savage spend his first night at the lighthouse?

6. Of what do the seven skyscrapers that are floodlit at night remind the Savage?

7. How is the Savage's place found?

8. What does the reporter from *The Hourly Radio* try to do? What happens to him?

9. What does Darwin Bonaparte do with his film of the Savage?

10. How does the Savage pay for what he sees as his final sin?

Answers

1. The Savage is purging himself with a mustard emetic to rid himself of civilization.

2. Bernard and Helmholtz leave the next morning for their exile.

3. The Savage plans to find an uninhabited place in England and exile himself because Mond won't send him to an island.

4. The Savage finds a deserted piece of seacoast on the south coast of England near Portsmouth.

5. The Savage spends his first night praying and mimicking a crucifixion in the form of vigil.

6. The seven lit skyscrapers remind him of cathedral spires or pinnacles of the Southwest, reaching toward heaven and God.

7. Three Delta-Minus land workers happen on the Savage when he is whipping himself.

8. The reporter tries to get an interview with the Savage, who kicks him in his backside.

9. Bonaparte makes his film into an instant hit feely, *The Savage of Surrey.* It results in more visitors to the lighthouse.

10. The Savage hangs himself from the highest point in the lighthouse.

Suggested Essay Topics

1. Mustapha Mond told the Savage that he wanted to go on with the experiment and would not exile him to an island. Using this as a basis for argument, how could the major events that occur during John's exile have been engineered by Mond to bring about what he knew would be the end?

2. Explain how the Savage uses physical punishment as a way to try to cleanse and purify himself of both societies that he has known.

Sample Analytical Paper Topics

The following paper topics are based on the entire book. Following each topic is a thesis and sample outline. Use these as a starting point for your paper.

Topic #1

In the foreword to his novel, Aldous Huxley states, "The theme of *Brave New World* is not the advancement of science as such; it is the advancement of science as it affects individuals." Demonstrate how the novel fulfills what Huxley says is his theme.

Outline

I. Thesis Statement: *Science as it affects individuals is the theme of* Brave New World.

II. Science has replaced the family unit.

    A. Embryos are developed in bottles.

    B. Children are raised and conditioned by the State.

III. Science has replaced religion.

    A. Religious symbolism has been reshaped to technological symbolism.

    B. Individuals have no reason for self-denial.

IV. Science has provided safe outlets for human desires and emotions.

    A. *Soma* placates anger, hostility, and want.

    B. Genetic engineering allows only the intelligence necessary for each caste and sub-caste to fill its place in society.

    C. Violent Passion Surrogate and Pregnancy Substitutes control the more troublesome human desires.

Topic #2

    "The people who govern the Brave New World may not be sane (in what may be called the absolute sense of the word); but they are not madmen, and their aim is not anarchy, but social stability." —Aldous Huxley

    Why is social stability judged to be so important? Illustrate with examples from the novel.

Outline

I.   Thesis Statement: *Societies that are stable within themselves do not have a reason for civil conflict or international war.*

II.   Stable societies do not engender the want and need of civil war.

    A. All is provided for everyone.

    B. There is no desire or want since all is available.

III.   Stable societies do not need to take from others.

    A. If all is provided, there is no need for war.

    B. Envy and greed are not necessary.

IV.   Firm, constant control by a few is necessary for a stable society.

    A. People must think they have all they need, whether they do or not.

    B. Control must seem to be magnanimous.

Topic #3

John the Savage is a combination of the two societies in which he exists. He is also an outsider in both. How does this make him the perfect foil to bring out the flaws in his new world?

Outline

I.   Thesis Statement: *As an outsider, John sees some of the paradoxes that exist in the New World.*

II. John sees religious influence in things although Mustapha Mond says that religion has become unnecessary.

    A. The sign of the T is made with reverence resembling the sign of the cross.

    B. The rites of the Solidarity Group resemble Christian communion rites.

    C. *My Life and Work* by Our Ford is designed to look like the Bible.

III. Linda has told John that the Other Place is the perfect civilization.

    A. John loses his identity as a person and becomes the Savage.

    B. John cannot stand the constantly repetitive faces of the lower Bokanovsky Group castes.

    C. John does not understand why books like Shakespeare's plays are not available even for the higher castes.

    D. John does not see that words like freedom have no meaning to any caste.

IV. "Nothing costs enough here." (The Savage)

    A. Social stability has caused man to lose his spirit.

    B. This New World has no place for martyrs or heroes: no sacrifice.

Topic #4

John the Savage uses three of Shakespeare's plays, *The Tempest*, *Romeo and Juliet*, and *Othello*, to express his emotions throughout the novel. Demonstrate how he uses certain words from the plays to express his thoughts.

Outline

I. Thesis Statement: *Because John's main reading has been from Shakespeare's plays, they influence how he views both his worlds.*

II. John thinks of the words of *Othello* when he sees Linda or Lenina in an unfavorable situation.

    A. Iago in *Othello* uses the basest words to describe Desdemona with her imagined lover.

    B. John sees his mother as the lowest of women because of her free and open sex with Popé.

    C. When Lenina relates to John in sexual manner, words describing women as whores come to mind.

III. When Bernard offers to take John to London, John uses Miranda's speech from *The Tempest* to describe what he thinks the New World will be.

    A. When John visits the Electrical Equipment Corporation (Ch. XI), "O brave new world...." sticks in his throat, causing him to vomit.

    B. By the end of the novel, John doesn't even try to think of Miranda's words to justify what he sees.

IV. When thinking of the romanticized Lenina, Romeo's words about Juliet fill John's mind.

    A. When John first sees Lenina at the Reservation, he thinks of Juliet.

    B. In London, when John thinks of Lenina as he wishes her to be, he uses words describing Juliet.

Appendix

Summaries of the Shakespeare Plays Referred to in *Brave New World*

Aldous Huxley's title for the novel comes from Shakespeare's play *The Tempest*.

Prospero, once the Duke of Milan, is deposed by his brother Antonio. Prospero and his two-year-old daughter are abandoned in a small boat at sea. They find an island to live on. Miranda grows up to be a lovely young woman who has no knowledge of the world. Her father uses his power as a magician to create a storm that brings a boat carrying his old enemies to the island so he can punish them for his exile.

Two supernatural characters become Prospero's slaves on the island: Caliban, the deformed and base son of a dead witch, and Ariel, a spiritual being who had been imprisoned by Caliban's mother. These are the only other two beings Miranda had known. When Miranda sees the various men who have come to the island, she says, "O brave new world." Prospero, who has worldly experience, replies, "Tis new to thee."

The play is judged to have been written in 1610–1611, and shows the inner nature of human beings revealed in crisis and change.

Throughout the novel, John the Savage is drawn to two plays of Shakespeare: *Romeo and Juliet* and *Othello*. *Romeo and Juliet* is a tragedy of two young lovers. Juliet is a beautiful, virginal 14-year-old. Romeo is the handsome teenage son of the Montague family, sworn enemies of the Capulets, Juliet's family. Romeo sneaks into a Capulet party. When he and Juliet see each other, they instantly fall in love. They secretly marry with the help of Friar Laurence. After spending their wedding night together, Romeo becomes entangled in a feud between the members of both families and kills a Capulet cousin. He is banished from Verona, and Juliet's parents betrothe her to another man, unaware of her secret marriage. Friar Laurence mixes a potion to put Juliet into a death-like sleep so Romeo can come to the family tomb and take her away. Various problems ensue and Romeo does not receive the plan. He comes to the Capulet family tomb to mourn his beloved, takes poison, and dies beside her. Juliet awakens to find her dead husband and kills herself with his dagger. Thus, they become victims of fate and their star-crossed lives.

The other play is *Othello*, a story of jealousy and betrayal. Othello is a Moorish general who has come up through the ranks in the army of Venice. He elopes with Desdemona, the daughter of a Venetian senator. Despite the fact that he is an outsider in his society because of his color and his less-than-noble birth, he and his wife are happy in the beginning. Othello's aide, Iago, hates and envies the general and feels slighted. He remains in Othello's service for the express purpose of destroying him. Using various innocent situations, Iago manages to convince Othello that his wife is in an adulterous affair with another officer. Many of Iago's speeches contain very explicit and degrading sexual language to create rage and jealousy in Othello's mind. Finally, in a fit of rage, Othello smothers Desdemona in their bed with her pillow. Othello commits suicide. There is a constant violation of trust throughout the play which upsets the characters and the society around them. The sacrifice of the major characters restores that balance.

SECTION FIVE

Bibliography

Baugh, Albert C., ed. *A Literary History of England.* 2nd ed. New Jersey: Prentice-Hall, 1948.

Boyce, Charles. *Shakespeare A to Z.* New York: Roundtable Press, 1990.

Cross, Arthur Lyon, Ph.D. *A Shorter History of England and Greater Britain.* New York: The MacMillan Company, 1955.

Engle, T. L., and Snellgrove, Louis. *Psychology Its Principles and Applications.* 9th ed. Orlando: Harcourt Brace Jovanovich, 1989.

Harrison, G. B., ed. *Shakespeare: The Complete Works.* New York: Harcourt, Brace and Company, 1952.

Huxley, Aldous. *Brave New World.* New York: Harper & Row, 1946.

———. *Brave New World Revisited.* New York: Harper & Row, 1989.

Hynes, Samuel. *The Auden Generation: Literature and Politics in England in the 1930's.* New Jersey: Princeton University Press, 1976.

Locher, Frances Carol, ed. *Contemporary Authors.* Volumes 85-88. Michigan: Gale Research Company, 1980.

Macrone, Michael. *Brush Up Your Shakespeare!* New York: Harper Collins, 1992.

Temple, Ruth Z., and Tucker, Martin eds. *Library of Literary Criticism: Modern British Literature.* Vol. II: H to P. New York: Frederick Ungar, 1966.